GROWING UP WESTERN

GROWING UP WESTERN

Recollections by

DEE BROWN   A. B. GUTHRIE, JR.

DAVID LAVENDER   WRIGHT MORRIS   CLYDE RICE

WALLACE STEGNER   FRANK WATERS

Foreword by Larry McMurtry

Edited and with Introductions by Clarus Backes

Alfred A. Knopf New York, 1990

THIS IS A BORZOI BOOK PUBLISHED BY ALFRED A. KNOPF, INC.

Copyright © 1989 by Earlene C. Backes
Photographs by Joe Backes copyright © 1989 by Joe Backes
All rights reserved under International and Pan-American Copyright Conventions.
Published in the United States by Alfred A. Knopf, Inc., New York,
and simultaneously in Canada by Random House of Canada Limited, Toronto.
Distributed by Random House, Inc., New York.

ISBN 0–394–57393–5
LC 89–45274

Manufactured in the United States of America
First Edition

*Frontispiece: A surprisingly contented looking burro gives
eight boys a ride near Bodie, California, in 1910. (Seaver Center,
Natural History Museum of Los Angeles County)*

The allure of the Old West, with its intriguing mixture of myth and reality, is something that always fascinated Clarus Backes, our father. In May 1987, he envisioned a book in which some of the great founders of American Western literature would write autobiographical stories about growing up in the West—in a time and place that had existed in their childhood but no longer exists in modern society. He would visit each writer and do an introduction to his piece, showing the contrast between the boy of the story and the man of today.

In October 1988, after nearly three years of battling with cancer, and one month short of this book's completion, our father died. His goal, to bring the Old West to life for a new generation, did not. We took up where he left off and finished the project.

It's not easy to fill the shoes of someone who has a lifetime of experience and dedication to the craft of writing, and a love and respect for an era that is gone. We have tried to remain faithful to our father's concept for Growing Up Western, *and have tried to produce a book that is in keeping with the extraordinary talent of its contributors.*

We would like to thank our aunt and uncle, Mryna and Christopher Carey, for their financial assistance, and all the other friends and relatives who gave of their ideas and support; our mother, Earlene, for her perseverance in keeping the book on track; our father's editor, Ann Close, for her understanding and constant reshuffling of deadlines; and Larry McMurtry for graciously lending his name and efforts, at short notice, to the anthology.

This book is dedicated to our father, Clarus Backes, a true believer in "family projects," the bravest man we've known, and our best friend.

Laura, Joe, and Michael Backes
March 1989

Contents

Foreword by Larry McMurtry / ix

Dee Brown / 3   It Was a Magical Time

A. B. Guthrie, Jr. / 37   A Small Town in Montana

David Lavender / 63   Bonanza Land

Wright Morris / 99   How I Put In the Time

Clyde Rice / 125   Leaving the Fold: A Boyhood in Oregon

Wallace Stegner / 153   Finding the Place

Frank Waters / 187   The Changing and Unchangeable West

Foreword

Growing up Western and growing up to be writers were not, at first glance, readily compatible fates for the seven men whose memoirs make up this engaging book. Had any one of them chanced to be born female, the two fates would clearly have been even less compatible.

The writers Clarus Backes wisely tempted into memoir are no longer exactly whippersnappers; all of them had seen the fine light of a Western day by 1910. The land was in some sense settled, the frontier in some sense closed, but many of the colorful and vigorous citizens who settled the land and closed the frontier were still very much in evidence. These men—A. B. Guthrie, Jr., Frank Waters, Dee Brown, David Lavender, Wallace Stegner, Wright Morris, Clyde Rice—were in a real sense children of the territory that Huck Finn proposed to light out to. Their forebears might have been farmers, cowboys, country teachers, miners, railroad men, but in every case the vistas these writers knew in their boyhoods were immense and nonsuburban, as would not likely be the case now.

One seldom hears it stated, but suburbs *do* have their virtues, quite a few of which are useful to writers or to people who are trying to become writers. Good schools, community colleges, and public libraries are three that come to mind. Writing starts with reading, after all; in places where there is little to read and too few people of intellect to stimulate and instruct, it may take most of a lifetime to arrive at the notion that one might be a writer. Witness Clyde Rice, whose first book was published when he was eighty-one.

Mr. Rice, I admit, is an extreme example, but the point stands: In the West in the early decades of this century it is safe to say that the notion that a normal person might normally seek a career in any of the arts did not enjoy wide currency. It took a rare individual even to glimpse such a possibility. The most elemental stage of the struggle for survival on the frontier had just ended—the Indians had stopped fighting and the grizzlies had been considerably thinned out—but the next stage, making a living in a country where there were no guarantees, took almost as much energy. Practicality reigned, and for good reason; one trained to be a printer (Dee Brown) or a newspaperman (A. B. Guthrie, Jr.) or a teacher (Wallace Stegner). The West had its landmarks, but they were physical, not cultural: buttes and canyons, not Harvard and Yale. Probably the strongest poetry that many of these men heard in their youth was the vivid poetry of place-names—the names on the land, as George Stewart called them—most of these the momentary inspiration of anonymous, temporary poets who were otherwise Indians, mountain men, railroaders, cowboys, salesmen, bartenders, or rogues.

The point, to restate it once more, is that an imaginative person born and raised in one of the many remote places in the American West in the first decade of this century or even later is likely to have had a long way to go before he or she gets to the book or the teacher or the school that can begin the process of education from which good writing eventually comes. It doesn't come from clouds, it comes from books, as several of the men recorded here have eventually said.

But a long way to go can also be a simple way, even an easy way. The desire to learn, both from life and from books, is one of the stablest and least burdensome desires. From that one can be led naturally to a fascination with the potential yield of one's own imagination, a kind of wheat field in which the harvest is measured in books and not in bushels.

The men we hearken to here have harvested much. Their energy, curiosity, and intelligence led them first along the main-traveled roads used by practical men but brought them finally to the great concourse of literature. Several of them spent a good part of their lives in what might be thought practical occupations; the arc of their careers more resembles Conrad's than that of his brilliant young friend Stephen Crane. Others, particularly Wallace Stegner and Wright Morris, sprinted toward the life of letters as soon as they could sprint, becoming internationalists in spirit while remaining partial to the West in their settings and subjects.

Looking at the books the seven of them have produced makes it clear that what the West first gave them was not libraries but landscapes. With some exceptions, place and not personality animates their early books; their work is testimony both to the great beauty of Western spaces and the Western sky and also to the compelling, often terrible, power this landscape exerts on individual humans and on the human communities that have to try to survive on those plains and deserts, along those rivers, in those mountains, beneath those skies.

Though the point is debatable, I think it is worth mentioning that these men, with a few others now dead, such as Vardis Fisher, were in a sense the first literary generation the settled West produced. With only a few exceptions, what the West yielded in the nineteenth century was mainly the literature of exploration; it might shade toward history in *The Oregon Trail,* toward comedy in *Roughing It,* toward inspired travelogue in Raphael Pumpelly, but it depended on newness and was mainly written by men who neither began nor ended their lives in the West. The West touched them, in some cases profoundly, but it did not develop them, as it did the writers who left their records of that development here.

It is to the credit of the editor that he chose his writers with such discrimination, and to the credit of the writers that they responded so well.

—Larry McMurtry

GROWING UP WESTERN

Dee Brown walking the rails near his home in Little Rock, Arkansas. (Photo by Joe Backes)

DEE BROWN

I spoke to Dee Brown a few days after Christmas, just prior to the start of the New Year, when the holidays were beginning to wind down but still held enough promise of relaxation to allow us an unhurried conversation. At one point it occurred to me that here was a man well-known as a Western writer, dealing with Western themes like the Indian wars, the railroads, the army forts, yet whose roots weren't entirely grounded in the West. Born in Louisiana in 1908, he was raised in Arkansas, familiar with its southwestern oil fields but not cattle ranches or other staples of the Western experience. I asked him what had brought him back to his current home in Little Rock, Arkansas.

"I partially grew up here," he responded, as though he really couldn't picture himself living anywhere else. He did admit that he had actually spent less time there than any other place he had ever lived, and that when it came time to retire, he and his wife had eliminated all of the popular havens, including Santa Fe and Florida (either too crowded or the weather was bad, the reasons are unimportant now), leaving Little Rock as the most appealing choice. When all was said and done it seemed the only logical place to be.

Maybe that exemplifies best where Dee Brown is standing at eighty after all this time as a Western writer. He has come full circle, in his writing, in his attitude, in his whole life, it seems. He always ends up finding himself back at the places he likes best, doing the things that come most naturally to him.

From the very beginning he cultivated a fondness for information, which served as the foundation for his career as a librarian and historical novelist. Growing up in Stephens, a booming oil town in southwestern Arkansas (relocating there with his mother and younger sister from Louisiana after the death of his father), he fed his imagination with dime novels of savage Indians (indisputable fact to a young boy) and honed his journalistic skills printing a small newspaper on a hand press with his cousin, using the local Boy Scout troop as his reporters. "It ran for several weeks, and then we got tired of it," Brown confessed. "Setting the type was too much work. Besides, there were other things to do."

For a young boy of twelve, this included baseball, working with his mother at the local post office, and watching all of the hustle and activity of the oil boom as it swept through his small town. It also meant time to write his first story, which he sent in to *Blue Book Magazine*'s short-short-story contest. They paid him the then impressive sum of one hundred dollars. "I had it made," Brown joked. "I've never had to work another day since then." His career as a writer was under way. Sort of.

"I did sell them three more stories over the next few years, and each time I slightly changed my name, to be sure they would take it. The contest was for amateurs, and I had become a professional."

It would be some time, however, before Brown began to write full-time. After high school and a short career as a typesetter and part-time reporter for a small-town newspaper, he found himself at Arkansas State Teachers College and had his first true introduction to the West through Dean McBrien, a professor of Western history there. McBrien took Brown on an automobile tour of historical sites and Indian battlefields throughout the plains one summer, and it rooted in the young student a deep fascination with the American West. In particular, viewing the site of a massacre of women and children on the Pine Ridge reservation in South Dakota, and the mass burial there, planted

Dee Brown at home.
(Photo by Joe Backes)

the seeds for Brown's best-known work, *Bury My Heart at Wounded Knee.*

Despite his love and respect for the American frontier, however, I was startled to learn that Brown's first book had nothing to do with the West. It was not, as any bibliographical listing will report, *Wave High the Banner,* the fictionalized biography of frontiersman Davy Crockett, published in Philadelphia in 1942 and well received by critics for a first novel. It was something quite different.

After his college years, Brown had spent time in Washington, D.C., working as a library assistant at the U.S. Department of Agriculture and absorbing the crazy atmosphere of business and politics in the nation's capital. He wrote a parody of government bureaucracy and sent it to Macrae Smith in Philadelphia. He thought he had it sold.

"A day or two after Pearl Harbor, the editor I'd been working with called me from Philadelphia and said he was coming to Washington on government business and wanted to meet me in the Willard Hotel. I said, 'What about?' and he said, 'I'll tell you when I get there.' So we met in the bar of the hotel and he said that he couldn't publish my book because of the war. He said that the country had to knuckle down and get behind the government, not make fun of it."

The editor went on to ask if Brown had any other projects in the works, and could they publish that instead. Brown mentioned his historical novel about Davy Crockett (hardly more than the germ of an idea at the time), and the book was sold. "They didn't dare not publish it," Brown said, laughing. And the first novel? "Never published, though now it would be dated. Of course, nowadays you can't burlesque the government anymore. It burlesques itself."

The time in Washington put Brown's research skills to use, as his work took him from the Department of Agriculture to the Department of War, and eventually to a job at the library of agriculture at the University of Illinois, where he had received his degree in library science. And his research abilities served him well as his writing career took off.

Brown has always considered himself more of a nonfiction than fiction writer. "Historical novelist" is a permissible title, though not one of his favorites. He has always been very meticulous about his details, and very careful to document all of his sources, a trait he admits he learned from Professor McBrien. Though there have been exceptions. "Sometimes there isn't enough material. There's a story there and you can't fill it in with facts, so you let your imagination run wild."

Many of Brown's books, both fiction and nonfiction, have received excellent critical praise for their accuracy and attention to detail. Some of his better-known works include *The Gentle Tamers: Women of the Old Wild West* (1958), a collection of anecdotes and biographies of several of the West's most outstanding and unusual women; *The Galvanized Yankees* (1963), a fascinating account of Confederate prisoners being put to use as Indian fighters by the government of the North during the Civil War; and *Hear That Lonesome Whistle Blow: Railroads in the West* (1977), in which Brown reveals the darker side of the American expansion by rail across the Indian territories and the destruction of the land that this caused. (It was such an unfavorable portrait of the railroads, in fact, that Brown was denied access to Union Pacific's archives for further research.) Brown's most famous work, however, was the culmination of research for several other books, and is considered by some to be a landmark in the field of American Indian history.

Bury My Heart at Wounded Knee: An Indian History of the American West was inspired in part by the battle sites Brown visited (and still visits, he told me), part by his exposure to Indian cultures as a student, and part by the amount of material he had gathered on Indian lore and experience. One of the most interesting facets of the material, he noted, was the similarity that many of the translated speeches (from Indian councils and the like) had to the King James version of the Bible.

Brown explained: "When I first came across these I didn't believe they were genuine. . . . I thought that they were the work of some romantic interpreter who had read the Romantic poets and decided that he would put these words into the mouths of the Indians." Much of his research was on Chief Joseph, the eloquent leader of the Nez Percé tribe. "His speeches are probably more poetic than most," Brown observed. Although Joseph had three different translators over a period of about twenty-five years (two of which, Brown claims, didn't really have much respect for Chief Joseph), all three translations of his speeches revealed the same poetic style. Convinced that the pieces were genuine, Brown was then led to compile the perspective of the Indians into a historical portrait of the West, which became a much-read best-seller, highly praised for the consistency of its vision. Brown revealed his method of keeping that vision to Anne Courtmanche-Ellis in an interview for the *Wilson Library Bulletin:* "I would tell myself every night, 'I'm a very, very old Indian, and I'm remembering the past. And I'm looking toward the Atlantic Ocean.' And I kept that viewpoint every night. That's all I did."

There have been many books after *Bury My Heart,* of course, including the historical novels *Creek Mary's Blood* (1980) and *Killdeer Mountain* (1983). But his famous best-seller exemplifies his attitudes and viewpoints on the West, a part of the country that even though he is not entirely native to, he considers a part of himself.

He has come full circle now, sharing his life with Sara, his wife of over fifty years, at his home in Little Rock, Arkansas. He doesn't write as much anymore, except in his head. "I won't really go to work on anything till somebody hands me a contract," he jokes. He spends his time with photography or studying the old maps he's collected over the years. "It's nice to have maps around," he says, "so I can see where things are."

Oftentimes he just walks by the railroad tracks along the Arkansas River, near his home. It's a stretch of the old Chicago, Rock Island and Pacific built in the 1890s. The worn rails and cinders pass by a clump of trees surrounded by a low fence, where supposedly (though Brown insists there's little truth to it) Chinese railway workers lie buried in a mass grave. There's no evidence to prove their existence. "Couldn't find any markers," Brown said. "I've been all over, looking to see if there's anything. Sometimes you see little clumps of gravel as if [something] had been dug up. . . ."

Whether it's in his thinking during a short stroll out his back door, or whether he's doing research for his next book, American history and Dee Brown are always going to be closely linked. He's never been able to get away from it and always finds himself back at the places where he began.

Dee Brown wouldn't have it any other way.

M.B., 1989

It Was a Magical Time

The town in which I spent my early years was in southwestern Arkansas, and I sometimes wondered if I was a southerner or a westerner. Relatives came to visit from deep in Louisiana and from far western Texas. The Louisianians kept out of the sun, wore dress-up clothes much of the time, and talked about timber and cotton. The Texans were sunburned, wore rough clothing except on Sundays, and talked about horses and cattle. My favorite was a Texas cousin three or four years older than I, although I was jealous of his ability to ride a horse barebacked better than I could ride one saddled.

In the years immediately after the First World War, the town was about as rural as any other contemporary American village of around a thousand inhabitants. Its crudities I was unaware of, having known few other places for comparison. It must have had some pastoral attraction because the chief surveyor, who laid out the railroad right-of-way and prospective town sites, chose that place to name for himself—Stephens. The railroad was the St. Louis Southwestern. Its four daily passenger trains and numerous freight trains connected us to the outside world. There was also a special night express that sped by without stopping. If one could keep awake until nearly midnight, the express could be seen streaking through the town with whistle moaning, and leaving a shower of sparks and a twinkle of red lights in its wake. Everyone said it was

*Local citizens enjoying the sun after a sudden rainstorm in
Smackover, Arkansas. This boom town was similar in appearance
to Brown's hometown of Stephens, twenty miles away.
(Courtesy of the Collection of John Meek)*

Flags and banners decorate a train carrying passengers to the 1910 Exposition in Little Rock. (University of Arkansas at Little Rock, Archives and Special Collections)

filled with money boxes and important people bound for Mexico City. If I had owned a fortune I would have given all of it to ride that train into the mystery-laden southwestern land.

Other special trains appeared from time to time to halt on one of the sidetracks, awaiting passage of a regular scheduled train. Among them were circuses and excursions, and during one exciting year, when I was eight or nine, there were carloads of soldiers wearing peaked khaki hats. They were going to the Rio Grande to hunt Pancho Villa. On one occasion the soldiers tossed packs of hardtack to us, some of which we kept for months as treasures. I would have given another fortune to go with the soldiers, although I had nothing against Pancho Villa. From what I had read in magazines of his adventures, I classed him with Robin Hood.

The trains also provided us with books. The town had no bookstore and the only library was a tiny collection in a closet of the public school. So it was

*Dee and Corinne ride
a rented burro at
Happy Hollow, Hot
Springs National Park,
Arkansas in the summer
of 1920. (Dee Brown
family collection)*

that the first literature about the Old West that I encountered was in the form of dime novels purchased from a butch boy, or newsboy, on a train. Until roads were improved in the early twenties, and families began to acquire automobiles, we went everywhere on trains—ten miles to a whistle-stop to visit farming relatives, or twenty-five miles to the county seat, where adult members of the party transacted some business or other and the young ones attended a silent movie.

When privileged to ride a train, I went in search of the butch as soon as it was in motion—that is, if he did not first come striding through the car, shouting his peanuts, candy, soda pop, and magazines. He usually kept his wares between two seats at one end of the smoking car, opposite the conductor's seat, a little nest of desirables, especially the dime novels. The paper covers were garish scenes of frontier mayhem—Buffalo Bill, Jesse and Frank James, and Deadwood Dick. If I had two dimes to spare I would always buy two, and get my fill of frontier mythology, of which I believed every word in those preteenage years.

I bought my first hardcover book at Hot Springs. My mother and my aunts went there occasionally to take the mineral baths, which they believed would keep everybody healthy. Sometimes they would take my younger sister and me, and a trio of young cousins. We could not have afforded these visits except that a relative lived there, and found places for everybody to bunk in her rambling old house. I loved Hot Springs and its tourist attractions but hated the baths and having to drink three cups of the sulfuric water every morning before breakfast. The journeys there by railroad were all-day ordeals for the complaining adults, but I looked upon the three transfers from one line to another over a distance of little more than a hundred miles as a series of grand adventures. After the highways were graded and graveled we began to travel there by automobile in about half a day. One of my uncles who did the driving would always stop a few miles outside Hot Springs and point out the spot where

A carriage driver pauses while crossing Flint Creek near Siloam Springs, Arkansas. The road is covered by what appears to be unusually high water. (Courtesy Arkansas History Commission)

many years before Jesse James had robbed a stagecoach. This, of course, added excitement to the journey.

As I noted, the Springs was where I bought my first bound volume, for perhaps twenty-five cents, in a secondhand bookshop. The title is long forgotten, but it was one of those wild concoctions about the American Indian wars, a few facts mixed with numerous gory inventions. I think it was the profusion of gaudy illustrations that attracted my attention—attacks on forts, arrow-studded corpses, old scouts being burned at the stake, or staked out over anthills, wagon trains surrounded by fierce-faced Indian warriors.

Before we returned home, I read it through, and could not wait to show it to my peers. Young folk read a great deal more in that time than now, but what they got from it was probably no more uplifting or true to reality than the movies and TV shows they absorb today. An awful lot of bad writing was published in those days when print was king.

The few books that we youngsters owned were passed around until they were literally worn out, and by summer's end my book of Indian war horrors was a bit shaken, but so were all the Zane Greys and Tarzans in our boys' own circulating library.

The public school I attended had no particular rules about the books we could bring to read during study periods. The teachers preferred us to borrow books from the tiny school library, but instead the boys brought their favorites and the girls brought theirs, passing them around as we did in the summer.

In the winter of the year that I turned twelve and was in the sixth grade, I witnessed my first book burning and was so horrified by the act that it has remained permanently fixed in my memory. One of the boys in my class asked me to bring the horrors-of-Indian-warfare book to school. I complied willingly, but I asked him to be careful and not to read it while Mr. Brennan was in the classroom. Mr. Brennan sometimes confiscated unassigned books and locked them in the teacher's desk, making it difficult to retrieve them.

Patrick Brennan was the school principal, a native of Ireland with a strong brogue, a burly man with a round flushed face. He taught all the mathematics classes, and every morning came to instruct us in beginning algebra, remaining through a study period. His method of instruction was to inspire fear. He would send us to the blackboard, present a problem in his deep doomsday voice, and then would watch us squirm while we tried to solve it. Because of the anxiety he inspired in me, I rarely ever solved a blackboard problem. When the allotted time ended, he would come tramping down the aisle, pointing out the stupid errors we had made, and then would ask that we present one of our hands palm up so that he might strike it a stinging blow with a twelve-inch ruler.

After algebra class on the day I brought the Horrors of Indian Warfare to school, I was studying for a geography test when I suddenly became aware of Patrick Brennan stalking slowly along the aisle across from me. He was approaching the desk of my friend, who, against my warning, was surreptitiously reading the Horrors behind his geography book, so engrossed in it that he was quite unaware that Brennan was behind and not in front of him.

A moment later, the Horrors was in Brennan's hands. After a glance at the contents, he turned and strode over to the big wood-burning stove, which was in full blast against the winter cold. Without hesitation he lifted the top of the stove and dropped the book into the inferno. To ensure rapid conflagration he opened the stove's damper.

I was stunned, enraged, made murderous. If ever a book needed to be burned, perhaps the Horrors was in a top category. But I could not believe it at the time.

A few days after my twelfth birthday an oil well blew in about three miles from town, the first oil strike in southwestern Arkansas. Within a few weeks it changed everything for everybody in the community. Oil boomtowns were the

The Brown family on the front porch of their home in Stephens, Arkansas.
Left to right: Elizabeth Cranford (grandmother), Dee Brown,
Lula Brown (mother), and Dee's sister, Corinne. Taken about 1920.
(Dee Brown family collection)

last manifestations of the old western frontier spirit of sudden wealth, wild actions, risk taking, violence, and sinful carryings-on. For several months I was right in the middle of the exuberant madness, delighted to watch the outside world swirl within our little town.

A few years before the oil discovery, my mother had moved to Stephens with my younger sister and me from a Louisiana sawmill town, after the death of my father. My father was in the timber business, and one afternoon when he entered the company commissary, he was stabbed in the back without warning by a drunken deliveryman for no apparent reason. One of my earliest and starkest memories, from the age of four, is of his being brought along the sidewalk into our house, lying upon a wide board lifted above the shoulders of six men, with my distraught mother walking alongside. At first it was believed he would survive, but he did not. The lifetime effects of this single senseless momentary act upon several human beings made me aware at a very early age of connections and uncertainties. Somewhat uneasily, I have always expected the unexpected.

To deal with this tragedy, I believe my mother adopted a philosophy of inevitability, perhaps predestination. She had a store of biblical quotations that she used to emphasize her statements, and was a firm believer in Emerson's essay "Compensation," which she once made me read. She was widowed at thirty-nine, a handsome woman with dark brown hair and sparkling dark eyes. She always held herself erect when walking or sitting, and kept her head high, as though daring the world to do its worst. She couldn't bear for anyone to feel sorry for her and her two children.

The second child was my sister, Corinne, more than a year younger than I. Until well into our school years, I always thought of her as being fragile (which she never was), with her curls and neat silk bows and rustling starched dresses. Until we were old enough to go to school, one of our grandmothers, a former schoolteacher, lived with us. She taught both of us to read before we entered school. While we were growing up, Corinne and I went through the usual sibling rivalries, each believing the other to be favored. After we went into the world on our own in different directions, we became supportive friends.

My mother moved from Louisiana to Stephens to be near her relatives. For a time she worked in the only dry goods store in town, and then when the local postmaster left office she applied for the position and was appointed postmistress.

Until the oil discovery, the only major problems facing the little post office were the seasonal arrivals of hundreds of bulky mail-order catalogs from Sears Roebuck and Montgomery Ward. Every family received one of each, most of them going out on the four rural mail routes. The mail carriers hated the catalogs almost as fiercely as did the local merchants. Some of the carriers used automobiles in dry weather; all used horse-drawn buggies when the roads were very bad, and one man sometimes resorted to horseback, with a pair of saddlebags for the mail. Whatever mode of transport was used, several days were required for delivery of all the catalogs.

Soon after delivery the recipients would begin ordering various items, stopping the carriers to buy money orders, and this always added hours to the daily runs. And then a few days later an abundance of parcel post packages would arrive, further burdening the carriers. In the 1930s George Milburn wrote a short novel, *Catalogue,* about this recurring phenomenon in a contemporary Oklahoma town; it is true in every particular.

My mother the postmistress assigned me various duties. One was to sweep the post office floors every afternoon after school. Another was to meet the early-morning passenger train before school and rush the first-class mailbag up the hill from the station to the post office. Still another was to deliver special delivery letters. The dime I received for delivering each letter was my pay for the other duties. Before the oil boom, only one or two special deliveries

An oil rig dominates the landscape and the laborer standing at the base of the tower. Near Smackover, Arkansas, in the winter of 1923. (Courtesy of the Collection of John Meek)

came each week, but a dime in the 1920s would buy more than a dollar will today.

With the coming of the oil boom and its hordes of strangers, the volume of mail exploded. Until the Post Office Department authorized an assistant, one of my aunts came to help sort the letters. Within a few days, several special deliveries were arriving with each mail, most of them addressed to strangers with no address other than the town. Fortunately school soon closed for the summer, giving me plenty of time to search for the addressees. I would start out at the Boggs Hotel, which had turned into a beehive of activity, the long porch and lobby filled with men wearing Texas hats, red corduroy shirts, and fancy boots. Then I would go on to the various boardinghouses, and to a growing tent city that had blossomed along the railroad track.

Most of the tents were probably army surplus, each occupied by one or two men. They were crowded into a grassy area that had been used in summers for religious revival meetings and traveling theatrical companies, under very large tents. At the height of the tent city's brief existence it must have been a couple of hundred yards long and fifty yards wide. Some of the occupants painted their names on the canvas fronts or on wooden stakes. When I went there to deliver letters I was usually welcomed as a bringer of news from outside. After dark, however, youngsters weren't allowed in the tent city. What went on there then was a subject of much conjecture among my peers, but the tent city was gone before we attempted a proposed stealthy reconnaissance.

Meanwhile the town was filling with the equipment and machinery of oil drilling. Long freight trains rolled into the railroad sidings to unload drilling rigs, steel pipes, lumber, stationary steam engines, and boilers. These were loaded upon the undependable automobile trucks of that time or upon the very dependable mule-drawn flatbed wagons. This traffic clogged the graveled streets and roads, which quickly disintegrated. After rains every road out of town became a bog, and as soon as the sun dried the mud it turned to powdered dust that smothered any traveler caught behind the caravans. Just outside town forests of wooden derricks soon replaced the forests of pine. Lights glimmered all night on the crown blocks, and the rackety clank and steady thud of drilling machinery never ceased.

Occasionally we walked or rode bicycles out toward Smackover Creek to watch the roustabouts struggle with the casing and rigging on the derrick floors. We were fascinated by the earthen slushpits, flowing with muddy water away from the well. If the well was nearing completion, the driller frequently would come out to the slushpit and thrust his fingers in it to smell and taste the flow. This wasn't a gusher field, but sometimes the first strike would shoot up to the crown block with a roar and then subside. The crude oil was dark brown—brown gold, the oil men called it—and its pungent aroma was not unpleasant. The smell of money, the oilmen said.

I soon learned that there were different classes of working oilmen—drillers, rig builders, and roustabouts. Drillers were the aristocrats, distinguishable by their diamond rings and stickpins and bright-colored silk shirts and neckties. Oil scouts wore sleek leather jackets. On the heels of these pioneers came the lease hounds, wildcatters, oil smellers or geologists, traders, and promoters. This later lot wore blue serge or seersucker suits. Almost all of them received special delivery letters, so that I was soon awash in dimes.

During the autumn several new students, children of the oil people, appeared at our school. In a seat next to mine was Bud Carnes, the son of an oil driller. I cannot recall his real first name. It was biblical, and he signed it on his school papers, but to his family and peers he was Bud. His complexion was olive and his facial structure slightly Indian. I never asked him about that, and we were close friends for several months before he shyly told me that he had Creek Indian blood. I had noticed that his mother was quite dark, but his father was not. Bud knew and I knew that some people with Indian blood tried to conceal it (in those days) out of fear of racial prejudice. Bud did not speak of it with pride, as I thought I would have done, but then I had never walked in his shoes.

Before the rapid increase in oil wells fouled all the nearby streams, Bud and I went fishing with hooks and worms; we took turns riding my uncle's old buggy horse; we climbed trees for wild grapes; we stole watermelons from farmers' patches. After a movie theater opened on Main Street we went to see the "Westerns" on Saturdays. One day when the audience was cheering cavalrymen who were slaying a band of Indians, Bud joined in the applause. Afterward I asked him why he would do that, being an Indian himself. With one of his rare smiles he replied: "Those were not real Indians. They were actors. If they were real Indians, I'd pitch in with them."

Sometime along at the height of the boom, the Stephens oil field began attracting a number of fast promoters and flimflam artists. A pair of oil-stock peddlers named Jimmy Cox and Doc Ladd were the most romantic of these people.

With their flair for the dramatic, Cox and Ladd disdained to come by way of the St. Louis Southwestern Railroad or by automobile. They arrived from Texas by airplane, in a Curtiss Jenny, a model they had flown during the First World War—which was then only four or five years in the past.

Being first-rate promotion men, Cox and Ladd notified our local weekly, the Stephens *News,* of the date and approximate time of their arrival in a cow pasture south of town. We had seen an occasional airplane flying high in the sky, following the railroad as was the practice in those days, but few of us had seen a plane on the ground. Consequently almost the entire town turned out for the arrival of Cox and Ladd.

The plane appeared so suddenly, swooping and hopping and rolling across the uneven surface of the pasture, that we scarcely had time to see or hear it before it was down. On the ground it resembled a fragile insect made of spruce, linen, and wire, leaping swiftly toward a grass-camouflaged ditch where its nose abruptly tipped forward, its tail pointing skyward. As we swarmed toward the plane, a spray of broken wood from a splintered propeller miraculously missed all of us.

We could see the leather-helmeted heads of the plane's two occupants. A slim man crawled out first, pushing his goggles back on his forehead. He wore a yellow silk scarf around his neck. Behind him was a stocky man who lifted a fat bulldog from the cockpit. He wore pants that flared at the hips and tightened at the knees, and his lower legs were encased in leather military puttees. The slim man walked around to inspect the broken propeller. He swore softly and said that they would have to telegraph Fort Worth for a replacement.

By this time some of the town's important men were pushing forward to welcome the arrivals, and we soon learned that the slender man was Jimmy Cox, the stocky man Doc Ladd. Within a few days Cox and Ladd and their bulldog had ingratiated themselves into the hearts of the citizens. They wasted no time hobnobbing with oil people like themselves. Instead they mingled with us, spending time with the town's business and professional men, and swapping stories with the local war veterans. Jimmy Cox walked with a slight limp, and everybody said he had been wounded in a dogfight with the German ace Richthofen, the Red Baron.

They opened a large account at the bank, and one day came into the post office, introduced themselves, and rented one of the two oversized mail boxes. The Stephens *News* rented the other one, but the second box had remained unrented until Cox and Ladd arrived. We all wondered why they would need such a large box.

Cox and Ladd soon opened a headquarters in a brand-new brick building on Main Street that some enterprising businessmen had rushed to completion. To occupy the desks, four or five young women arrived suddenly one day from

A man and his wife prepare to clean a string of freshly caught fish in Sulphur Springs, Arkansas. The clouds are obviously hand-painted by the photographer. (Arkansas History Commission)

Texas. I thought they were the prettiest females I had ever seen. They wore jaunty tam-o'-shanters, low-cut shirtwaists and skirts short enough to expose half the calves of their white-stockinged legs. They also used considerably more rouge than did the local girls.

Two of these glamorous office workers came into the post office one day and startled my mother by asking for ten thousand penny postcards. Only a few hundred cards were in stock, of course, but within a week the ten thousand were obtained. Cox and Ladd rushed them over to the Stephens *News* job press and shortly afterward they were brought back to the post office for mailing. They contained an exciting message composed by Jimmy Cox, and were addressed to people all over the country, the majority going to California. Many of the addressees had "Dr." before their names, and I understand that to this day doctors and dentists still have a weakness for hot oil stocks. For that is what Cox and Ladd were selling.

Large bundles of first-class letters followed the postcards, and then a special edition of the Stephens *News,* containing a two-column article describing Cox and Ladd's glorious oil enterprises, written by the former. Needless to say this avalanche of postcards, letters, and newspapers (which were rolled in penny wrappers) created a problem for the post office. We had only one hand stamp canceler, and not only I but all the rural carriers took turns canceling the drift heaps of outgoing mail.

Jimmy Cox wrote all the oil-stock sales copy, and I believe his was the first writing style I attempted to imitate. In fact I was not aware that there was such a thing as a writing style until I read the literary compositions of Jimmy Cox. He kept his relationships with his clients on a highly personal level, greeting them as "pardners," confiding in them his discovery of what might be the largest "mother pool" of oil in the world, and giving them the first chance at a once-in-a-lifetime opportunity to make a fortune beyond their wildest dreams. He assured them that Cox and Ladd could dive deeper and come up with more oil profits than any wildcatters in the business. For a limited time only, the inside "pardners" could send a check for one share, ten shares, a hundred shares, or more, before this opportunity for sure riches would be opened to the general public. The complimentary close to his message struck me as being a piece of literary genius: "Fortune smiles but tempus fugits."

Not long after the first series of mailings went out, a flood of letters began arriving from California and elsewhere, each mail filling up Cox and Ladd's big box. A surprising number came special delivery. To earn four or five dollars (a fortune in the 1920s) all I had to do was walk around the corner, enter the new brick building on Main Street, and hand a packet of letters to one of the spicily perfumed young women in the offices of Cox and Ladd.

But it was too good to last. One morning when I reported for special delivery duties, I found my mother and her assistant in a state of high excitement. They had received a telegram from the inspection division of the Post Office Department stating that a fraud order had been issued against Cox and Ladd. Their box was to be sealed, and all their mail held pending arrival of a postal inspector.

Although none of us realized it at the time, the downfall of Cox and Ladd symbolized the end of the oil boom at Stephens. Bigger strikes were being made some miles to the east. The drillers, roustabouts, scouts, and promoters flocked away to wild places like Smackover and El Dorado, leaving our town in a state of suspension. The number of special delivery letters dropped back to one or two a week. The offices of Cox and Ladd were closed, they too departing to new fields to prospect while awaiting trial for their oil-stock scheme.

Regardless of what wrongs that pair may have committed in their merry and swaggering appeals to mankind's natural greed, they had brought into our placid lives more color and glamour than had ever touched us before. For me they will always be men of magic, true artists at their trickster games.

A noontime view of busy Main Street in Little Rock, looking toward a bridge crossing the Arkansas River. (University of Arkansas at Little Rock, Archives and Special Collections)

The end of the oil boom also signaled the end of my life at Stephens. The town turned drab in its shrinking; the streams and much of the vegetation were fouled. Several of the best teachers left our school. After a visit to a sister in Little Rock, my mother decided to move there, so that my sister and I could attend a better school.

And so at the age of sixteen I began life in a city, not large, but for me a place filled with many wonders, and although I lived there but three years, it was a bonding time. No matter my long absences and far distances away, Little Rock has always been my hometown.

Several significant events that were to shape my future occurred during those three teenaged years. I took all the courses in trade printing offered by the high school so that I was equipped to earn a living when I graduated. I learned to play baseball, my favorite game because more than any other it simulates the triumphs and failures of individuals acting in concert. Baseball brought me in touch with Moses Yellowhorse, Pawnee Indian and fastball pitcher for the Arkansas Travelers. He made me believe in the kindness and generosity of American Indians. I encountered a three-volume work: *History of the Expedition Under the Command of Captains Lewis and Clark,* and discovered the real American West. It was far more exciting than any dime novel, or even Stevenson's *Treasure Island,* which it somewhat resembles in style and structure and suspense. In my last year in high school I wrote my first short story (about baseball) and sold it to *Blue Book Magazine* for what I considered to be a fabulous sum.

And then I graduated from high school and found a job as a printer on the Harrison *Times,* deep in the heart of the Ozarks. After a few months I was a part-time linotype operator and part-time reporter. I became a reporter by accident. When a tornado ripped through the neighboring town of Green Forest, I joined a group of young men who piled into a truck to go to the aid of the victims. We worked all night, lifting debris and searching for dead and injured among the devastated buildings. At sunrise an eerie scene unfolded: half the town was untouched, the other half desolate. We made a wider sweep through the fields and battered woods around the town.

Late in the morning I suddenly realized that I was supposed to be at my linotype, setting copy for the afternoon daily. The truck that had brought us had disappeared, but a passenger train was standing at the railroad station. It brought me into Harrison less than an hour before press time. My boss, the editor, was only slightly peeved. He had guessed the reason for my absence, and all morning had been helping with the typesetting. The press service had wired a two-sentence bulletin about the tornado, but he wanted more than that. "You were there," he said gruffly. "Write it."

He never commented upon my hastily composed account of the tornado, but after that he began sending me out on special assignments. The full-time local reporter, an earnest young woman, disliked violence, and so I was given the accidents and shootings, the mountain feuds.

And then in my second summer, a local boy who was a college student began working part-time on the paper. By September he had convinced me that I, too, should go to college, and so off we went to the teachers college at Conway, in the Arkansas River valley.

The morning that I first set foot on the campus, I was greeted by a man who appeared to be no more than five or six years older than I. He was a good five inches shorter, but his head was massive, his hair close clipped, his eyes very sharp and penetrating, as he extended a hand and introduced himself in a gravelly voice as Professor Dean McBrien. The meeting was providential. McBrien was a professor of history, fresh from the University of Nebraska, an enthusiastic student of Western American history.

Dean McBrien more than any other mentor set me upon the course I was to take as a writer. He probably did not care very much for the historical novels I later published, but he could not help but like my way of writing history,

Dee Brown (in hat) and Professor McBrien leaning against a petrified log in the Kaibab forest. Taken in 1931, when Brown was twenty-three. (Dee Brown family collection)

because I borrowed or stole the methods he used in his classes to charm his students into attentive listeners.

McBrien's view of history was that the past consisted of stories, fascinating incidents, woven around incisive biographies of the persons involved in the happenings. He liked little dashes of scandal—if they could be documented— and he insisted firmly that everything had to be authenticated from the available sources. He had saturated himself in the history of the American West. Before I met him, I was interested in the American West, but he converted me into a fanatic like himself.

Almost every summer during those years, he traveled across various parts of the West, usually with two students as companions. On two of these expeditions I was privileged to be invited, and learned far more than any classroom could offer. McBrien preferred to travel in a Model T Ford. Although the Model

An early touring car makes time across the Colorado plains with the snow-covered Rockies looming in the distance. (Courtesy local history collection, Pike's Peak Library District)

A had replaced the Model T, the latter was still available for a few dollars in various used conditions. Before I was nineteen I owned or shared ownership in three different rattletrap Model T's, and I had always accepted them as a part of the natural environment.

McBrien, however, made me see them for the remarkable machines they were, comparing them to the living, breathing steam locomotives that were beginning to pass from the railroads. When one cranked a Model T into life, it would nudge forward like a friendly horse eager to be in motion. If the motor had been badly treated so that the spark lever had to be pushed down to make it start, the crank would kick, sometimes so hard the thrust could break a wrist. If a Model T stopped running, a ten-year-old could repair it, and drive it. If a tire blew out, the casing could be stuffed with dried grass or pine needles and put back on the road. If the radiator sprang a leak, a small bag of cornmeal poured inside would cure the ailment in five minutes. Because Model T touring cars moved slowly, were open to the sun and wind, and afforded a perfect view of the landscape, Dean McBrien believed them superior to all other means of traversing the West.

On our journeys he never forced upon us his knowledge of events that had occurred in the places where we traveled, but if we gave him an opening—and we usually did—he would respond with one of his delightful little incidents, accompanied perhaps by an incisive biography, all laid out for us right where it had happened.

When I hear that old adage about a good teacher needing only a simple bench with the teacher at one end and the student at the other, I want to amend it to the front seat of a Model T Ford with the student at the wheel and the teacher at his side, unlocking the past and relating it to present and future.

Perhaps because he was a Nebraskan, McBrien was fond of the Great Plains and refused to hurry across them, as so many travelers do, and I learned to admire the vast distances and enormous bowl of sky that would swirl above us with the passage of the slow-moving car. He must have read every overland diary and narrative then available, and would insist upon stopping for hours to examine places along the Oregon Trail, which we followed one summer.

These journeys and others that I later undertook on my own formed a basis for most of the books I would write. That time was more than half a century ago, a time not too distant from the years of cattle drives and the last Indian wars. We traveled mainly over unpaved roads across landscapes little changed from those of the nineteenth century. We had many small adventures, meeting inhabitants of small towns and Indians on reservations who remembered the great events of that earlier time.

When a person who is cognizant of a recorded incident of history first comes upon the place where it occurred, the impact can have the force of an exhilarating electrical surge. I remember a strange prickly sensation when, at twenty-one, I first saw the rude monument of stones beside the Bozeman Road in Wyoming, the marker for the Fetterman fight of 1866. This was a victory for the Plains Indians—Sioux, Cheyenne, and Arapaho—sometimes credited to the leadership of Red Cloud, who demanded abandonment of forts along the Bozeman Road before he would sign the "lasting peace" treaty at Fort Laramie. The Fetterman fight would loom much larger today in the annals of Indian wars had the Little Bighorn not overshadowed it ten years later.

I knew that something shattering had occurred there and from around the site of the vanished Fort Phil Kearny, along the rim of deceptive ridges, to the brooding Bighorn range, misty and cloud-covered that day. The air was filled with courageous spirits of the past, red-man spirits, white-man spirits.

The Custer battlefield struck me somewhat in the same way, but because we knew so much about it the place wasn't as compelling as the hidden enigmas of Fort Phil Kearny. Thirty years later I thought I knew enough to write about it.

The sites of old Fort Wallace and Beecher Island would have been insignificant without the legends in our heads. Fort Wallace, in far-western Kansas, had already vanished, leveled by time, when we visited the site. Wallace, the railhead that supplied the fort, was a ghost town. They were booming centers of military action and commerce in the years immediately following the Civil War. Custer used the fort as a base in 1867. Lieutenant Frederick Beecher left there in 1868 to cross into Colorado and meet his doom on an island in the Arikaree. When we found the place, Beecher Island had been erased by river currents, but the ghosts of Roman Nose and the dead frontier volunteers were still there.

In those useful years of searching, the most painful place we came upon was a mass grave with a few flowers struggling to live around it, in South Dakota, Pine Ridge reservation. A monument bore the names of some Indians, but most of those buried there were unrecorded and unknown—men, women, and children, killed at Wounded Knee. That grave remained like the scar of a wound imprinted forever upon me.

I am glad that I first saw all these and other places in the American West while they and I were still young. I am glad I grew up when and where I did. Even with all its calamities and woes, that brief time may have been the best time to be alive in the entire era of our Republic.

*A. B. Guthrie, Jr., with Ear Mountain
in the background. (Photo by Joe Backes)*

A. B. GUTHRIE, JR.

In the end, what Bud Guthrie did is exactly what boys growing up in country towns have dreamed of doing probably since civilization began: He ventured forth into the big world out there and made a success of himself, then came in triumph back home. Home to little Choteau, Montana (population 1,798), a stone's throw from the Teton River in the shadow of the northern Rockies. To a house he built himself on eight hundred acres of sagebrush and scrub pine and calls The Barn, because from a distance it looks like exactly that, designed as a replica of the traditional, splayed-roof Montana outbuilding that housed the horses on his father's place so many years before. He has lived there now for more than twelve years with his wife, Carol, his many mementos, a playful half-poodle, half–cocker spaniel named John Hall Goddam His Eyes and assorted passing skunks, badgers, bears, and mule deer.

But the reasons for his return aren't quite what one might suppose. There are no longer, after all those years, parents or siblings left around for him to be close to; his kid brother Chick, a popular, longtime columnist for a Minneapolis newspaper, died in 1975, and his only remaining sister, Janie, followed in 1987. Nor are there old friends left nearby to impress. Even the Choteau party days—and there were a few of those, mostly in joyous celebration of one literary triumph or another—are a thing of the past. Rather what drew him and continues to hold him, he says, is the land itself—the perfect, peaceful solitude the land offers. That and the feeling all around that he is standing directly in the channel flow of passing history.

There is, for example, evidence that once, thousands upon thousands of years ago, there was considerable human traffic following a well-traveled route nearby. According to a historical marker planted beside the county road: "Through this immediate region, hard by the mountains, ran the Old North Trail, its starting point far to the north, its termination far to the south, its origins lost in the mists. It is a surmise that long-ago Mongols crossed the Bering Sea land bridge, found and marked their way south and became, or merged with, our Indians of mountains and plains. History runs into mystery here."

It is only one of many signs of prehistoric activity near the Guthrie place. Less than ten miles away paleontologists recently uncovered a large graveyard of duck-billed dinosaurs—adults, infants, nests, and eggs—dating from more than seventy million years ago. There is an old buffalo jump closer still, where long-ago Indians once herded the panicky animals off the edge of a cliff, then butchered the dead and dying below.

"It gives me a chill sometimes to go walking and come across an arrowhead or a piece of dusted bone—and they're all around here," says Bud. "It makes me feel like I'm a part of something that's been going on for a long time."

But Carol, listening, shrugs this bit of sentimentality off. "He came back because of the mountain," she says. "Over there." She gestures toward a peak in the mountain range rising abruptly from the prairie floor out the sun-room window, seemingly only a short stroll away. "He wanted to be near it again."

And Bud nods in placid agreement, caught out.

Oh, yes. The mountain.

As peaks go in this part of the Rockies, it doesn't look especially magnetic. Just another mountain, really—an outcropping of gray, largely lifeless stone. Because at certain times of day the sunlight creates dark shadows on it that

A. B. Guthrie, Jr.
(Photo by Joe Backes)

suggest the flaring, erect ear of an African elephant, locals have long called it Ear Mountain, although the name doesn't appear on any map. It stands eighty-five hundred feet high, a few hundred feet higher than the peaks on either side of it, rising some four thousand feet above the eastern Montana plateau.

The Blackfoot Indians, however, regarded the mountain as sacred; near its top is a vision-quest site—a small, cleared area surrounded by a kind of low wall where Indian boys used to come to undergo the tribal manhood rite. Bud and Carol looked down on the place once from a small plane; few white people have had the stamina or compelling curiosity to make the climb on foot. The Indian boys would remain there for days without food or water, Bud explained, seeking some mystical message, and finally would grow faint and begin to hallucinate. Inevitably, at this most impressionable time, a sign would appear—a soaring eagle, a curiously shaped cloud—that would not only offer them a guideline for their future behavior but would also provide them with that most basic of necessities, a suitable name to carry through adult life.

Bud, an avowed antireligionist, relates this with some feeling. "Why not?" he asks almost pugnaciously. "It makes at least as much sense as anything I've heard coming out of a so-called civilized church. Don't you agree?"

He is, even at eighty-seven, a man full of fight, the passions of a lifetime still setting off rockets within him. Once, during the two days we spent together, I took issue with his objections to the new, computer-aided research being conducted on the nearby Custer battlefield. He turned to me with fire in his eyes. "We should let the dead rest. It's just morbid curiosity. Give me one good reason for wanting to know more than we already do about what went on there. Just one," he demanded.

Well, I ventured timidly, it seemed to me that if we knew for certain how Custer's men behaved under the circumstances they were in, instead of just guessing about it, it might reveal something to us about ourselves. About human nature in general . . .

"Now that's a perfectly valid reason to me," Carol said, jumping in, obviously knowing the danger signs better than I did and doing her best to head off calamity. "Don't you think so, honey? I can certainly go along with that."

"Humph," Bud replied.

But if he can be passionate, Guthrie can also be exceedingly gracious. He and Carol host frequent out-of-town guests, especially on the weekends, even in the midst of Montana's brutal winters; a constant stream of editors, historians, novelists, and just plain good friends have managed to buck the snowdrifts and find their way there. He also has become something of a literary godfather and a good friend to other, younger novelists and poets he admires who have drawn their material from the Montana region, people such as Ivan Doig, James Welch, and the late Richard Hugo.

Life indeed appears good these days, a succession of long, productive afternoons at the typewriter (he was deep into work on a new novel) and peaceful, star-filled nights at home (he and Carol love to lose themselves in books, often reading until 2:00 A.M.). But such was not always the case. Guthrie's literary career, in fact, was anything but instant, or even entirely foreseen.

After working as a boy for the Choteau *Acantha,* a local weekly his father had once owned, and graduating finally from the University of Montana with a degree in journalism, Guthrie set out in 1923 determined to make his mark in the big-time newspaper world. But there was a recession on; moreover, Cornelius Vanderbilt, Jr.'s, Los Angeles tabloid had recently folded, flooding the market with experienced reporters competing aggressively for the few available jobs. So Bud ended up instead working on a rice farm in Mexico, for a grocery-store chain in California, for the U.S. Forest Service in Montana, and finally for an uncle's feed mill in upstate New York. It wasn't until 1926, after the feed mill suddenly burned down, that he managed to get his foot inside a newspaper at all. Then he landed a job as a cub reporter for the Lexington *Leader* in Kentucky.

He remained there for twenty-one years, moving up the ladder to reporter, city editor, editorial writer, and finally executive editor. In 1943 he published a detective novel with a Western setting, *Murders at Moon Dance,* which he had begun working on seven years before. "In the absence of entire evidence I can't say it's the worst book ever written, but I've long considered it a contender," he was to admit later. Nevertheless it got him to thinking about the life of an author. It didn't seem like such a bad thing.

Then in 1944 he was awarded a Nieman fellowship for a year's study at Harvard, and used the time to write *The Big Sky,* the novel widely regarded as his masterpiece. It deals with the brief era of the fur-trapping mountain men between the years 1830 and 1843 and serves as the opening episode in his continuing fictional study of the development of the American West, which has since spread to five more volumes: *The Way West,* about life on the Oregon Trail; *These Thousand Hills,* concerning the cowboy and cattle ranching; *Arfive,* about the founding of a small Western town; *The Last Valley,* which explores the West in the period between the two world wars; and *Fair Land, Fair Land,* which fills a gap in the story between the second and third books.

The Way West was awarded the Pulitzer Prize for Fiction in 1950, the first of a long series of awards, honors, and honorary degrees to descend upon Guthrie. By then he had quit newspapering for good and was already having a high old time writing exactly what he wanted to write, not only for book publication but also for the popular magazines of the day and for the movies (he did the screenplay for *Shane* and the excellent *The Kentuckian,* among others). Living the kind of life they used to do picture spreads in the *Saturday Evening Post* about.

And now he is back right where he started from. He and Carol and John Hall.

A slender chapbook titled *Four Miles from Ear Mountain,* published in a limited, signed edition recently by the Kutenai Press of Missoula, contains this poem, which Guthrie wrote in 1986:

> *Ear Mountain stands four miles away,*
> *crow-flight, from our house.*
> *No day passes but I gaze on it*
> *as my father did when I was young.*
> *I see him looking out the window west,*
> *his eyes fixed and his body still.*
> *Restive, he found peace there perhaps,*
> *or in it some continuation of himself,*
> *some promise of foreverness.*
> *I did not know his thoughts,*
> *nor am I clear about my own*
> *as its lift invites my eye,*
> *and somehow I am part of it,*
> *a mortal partner to eternity.*

Yes, a kind of eternal partnership, that's what the mountain offers. It does seem reason enough for coming back.

C.B., 1987

Farmers work their fields in the Western plains with steel-tired, horse-drawn machinery, within view of the nearby mountains.
(Courtesy Special Collections, University of Nevada-Reno Library)

A Small Town in Montana

I grew up with the open outdoors all around me. Just out the windows, through the entrances, there it was with all its wonders. Five miles to the south, beyond the cluster of buildings that composed our little town, rose two buttes. They appeared so close in that clear air that a visitor from Indiana once proposed a stroll to them before breakfast. To the west, twenty miles distant, rose the ragged wall of the Rocky Mountains, and to the east and north distance swam to eternity, broken to the north on bright days by the blue shadows of the Sweetgrass Hills on the Canadian border.

Our town was Choteau, population then about 1,200, in north central Montana. On the eastern skirt of the place Spring Creek ran, and, to the west somewhat farther away, the Teton River. Willows and cottonwoods bordered the streams, and trout swam in blue holes, and on the way to the river were old buffalo wallows and sometimes a skull, and picket-pin gophers chirped in the grasses.

That was my town, that was my country, in the years from about 1901 to about 1919. It is the early part of that period, the young boyhood time, that concerns me here.

My father, reared on an Indiana farm, always kept a cow and a flock of chickens. The cow had to be a Jersey, by George, and the chickens silver-laced Wyandottes.

Bud's mother, June, and his sister Nina Bess in the backyard of the family home in Choteau, Montana. (From the Guthrie family collection)

I remember one cow from my earliest days. She was already old, too old to freshen, and in those last years gave no more, even less, than half a gallon of milk. But what milk! When it had cooled, the cream skimmed off in heavy folds, like soft leather. Mother made her own butter in a churn with an up-and-down paddle and often had skimmed milk on the stove for the making of cottage cheese. We loved the rich buttermilk. The like of it is not to be found anymore.

There came a time when Old Boss could hardly get about and produced barely a squirt of milk, and one afternoon my father got out his Winchester 97 twelve-gauge shotgun and said, "Come along, son." We went outside to the shed then and my father scooped up a half can of middlings, a stock food somewhere between bran and flour. He dumped it in the feed trough and let the cow gum away, saying nothing. When she had finished, he put a rope around her neck and set out, going slow for her sake. A gentle creature, she ambled along as best she could.

About a mile west of our house, out in the buck-brushed open, Father halted, took the rope from the cow's neck and stepped in front of her. She waited. He pumped a shell in the chamber, pointed the gun at her head and for an instant hesitated. Then the roar of the shot tore the quiet air, and Old Boss went down without a sound. I never knew why Father wanted me there.

But youngsters forget. Bad things become matters of curiosity. So it was that I sometimes took friends my age to see what remained of Old Boss. Our dog, a Gordon setter named Jimps, rolled in the decaying carcass in spite of my shouts and arrived home stinking. On those occasions I didn't nap with her behind the wood-and-coal range.

Other cows came and went, but never another like Boss. Several other householders kept cows, for no real dairy existed and not yet, in early 1900, was milk available in stores. A cow necessitated a back lot, of course, and we had a big one. After the morning's milking the cows were turned out in the summertime, turned out on the town to go where they would. They had a habit of going south, to open and grassy pastures, and we sons of their owners and our friends walked out to get them in the early evenings. It was no chore. We lazed them home, pegging rocks at gophers as we went.

Gardens were numerous, too, short though our growing season was. Fenced in against the cows, they produced quite an assortment of vegetables including, late in the season, a variety of roasting ears that we called squaw corn. No tomatoes, though, but cabbages, potatoes, turnips, string beans, and early growing radishes and lettuce. Once in a while a gate was left open. Once in a while a section of fence fell over, and then an anguished cry would sound in the house. "There's a cow in the garden." All hands ran out to chase the cow off and assess the damage.

We were proud of our chickens. Nothing compared with those Wyandottes, and no other compared with a rooster that my father had sent away for. One day, returning from what was probably the second grade, I found our bird standing bloody but combative over a collapsed Rhode Island Red. I picked him up and cleaned him off as best I could. Next day in school I hugged the thought of him to me, my heart quick in my chest. A battling rooster! Who cared for phonics when a fight was in prospect? Thereafter at the end of classes I ran home, scooped up my Wyandotte, and, traveling back alleys, introduced him to other flocks and other roosters. Then I lay, hiding, my breath short, and watched. My bird always won. I took him under my arm then, carried him home, and gave him an extra feeding of wheat. After three battles we ran out of nearby opponents, and I retired him as grand champion, never defeated.

I could identify every hen in our flock, as could my younger brother, Chick. Once, poking along the Teton, I found a mallard's nest. I took the ten eggs and put them under a broody hen. They hatched out, cute but unruly, and soon found the irrigation ditch that served our lawn and garden. I have a mental picture of the hen, running along the bank trying to cluck them

Chick, left, Nina Bess, and Bud play in the car of a family friend about 1909. Less than four years later Nina Bess was dead of meningitis. (From the Guthrie family collection)

ashore. One day hen and ducklings disappeared, never to be seen again.

We had horses, too, one at a time and one that will remain forever in memory. A handsome beast, trained both for buggy and saddle, he was gentle but spooky. The slightest thing made him shy. Early in our experience with him my sister and I had been reading *Black Beauty,* with its emphasis on cruelty to animals. One of the cruelties was blinkers on bridles. Why, the poor horse couldn't see to the side much less behind him. At our urging and against his better judgment, Father cut off the blinkers. Then, a day or two afterward, we planned to take a drive, all of us, Father, Mother, and three children. Father hitched up. We got in the buggy. Father tapped Old Fox's rump with the reins and said, "Get up." Old Fox took a step or two and then saw that something was following him, something right on his heels. With an explosion of wind that could be heard for miles, Old Fox leaped into a run. Around the lot we tore, Mother hanging on to little Chick, Father sawing at the reins, sister and I grabbing for handholds. On the second turn around the lot, Fox tangled a shaft in the fence and came to a stop, trembling violently. We didn't go for that planned drive. Somehow *Black Beauty* disappeared from the house.

Periodically Old Fox would disappear, escaping through an open gate or a weakness in the fence. We knew his habits. He would look up his friend, a black gelding owned by the Cole family, who would manage his own freedom somehow, and they'd make for the open Freezeout country fifteen or so miles south of town. At intervals the young men of the vicinity would organize a small-scale horse roundup and return our animals. One such buckaroo told me that Old Fox was the toughest bucker in the whole bunch they'd found. That was fine with me. Riding bareback with a willow switch in one hand, I'd urge Old Fox on, riding proud, riding on the prize bronc.

In those early years my father liked to fish and to hunt. I used to wait for his return, then count and exclaim over the trout or, in hunting season, smooth the feathers of prairie chickens or ducks. In my turn I became angler and hunter. My first rifle was a single-shot Stevens .22 with, as I was proud to point out, an ivory bead for a front sight. It was some time before I was allowed to go afield with it and longer yet before I shot anything but gophers. Meantime I'd go with my father, fishing or hunting depending on the seasons. He knew or had learned how to handle a fly rod. He cast delicately, and the fly hook fluttered on the water like something alive. I rejoiced when he landed a fish.

With hunting season at hand we'd hook up Old Fox and set out. One favorite spot was Cashman Coulee, where potholes usually were good for three or four teals. I drove the horse when Father took off to hunt. Old Fox trembled at the sound of a shot and sometimes kicked and got a kick in the belly in return when Father returned and got too close, his hunting coat smelling of blood and spent powder.

Above the rise from Cashman Coulee were three small lakes about a half mile apart. Father would unhook Old Fox, tie him to a wheel, and set out decoys in the biggest of the lakes. Then he'd put on a grass suit—I've never seen or heard of another one—and, crouching, would look like a shock of wheat. It was my job to run between the two other lakes and flush any ducks there, the aim being to get them circling above the decoys. I'd hear the gun boom and feel good, and once from a rise saw smoke from a shot before I heard the explosion—my introduction to the difference in speed between sight and sound.

My parents had lost four babies from one disease or another, and Mother was always fearful for the rest of us. It was with anxious reluctance, until we got older, that she allowed us to go swimming without an adult in attendance. When she did let us, it was with the injunction that we were not to go into water over our heads. It was easy to obey in shallow Spring Creek, where the deepest pools were no more than breast high. We had fine times, though I tremble to think of them now. We turned blue with the cold of that water. Our skin crimped. Our bones ached. We shivered. We ran from the swimming hole to the fire we'd prepared on the bank. Warmed up, we plunged into that killing water again.

Sometimes we combined swimming with a kind of fishing. We snared suckers or whitefish. We had cane poles or, in their absence, fresh-cut willow ones. To each we'd fasten a length of copper wire with a running loop at the end. In clear water it was easy to slip the noose over a fish, tighten it with a jerk, and yank the fish out. They weren't worth eating. We never carried them home, just let them lie.

*Chick, left, and Bud proudly help their father display the day's catch
near the Teton River in 1912. (From the Guthrie family collection)*

I have always liked solitude, if not as a constant companion. As a fourth grader, I used to look out the school window and gaze on Cashman Coulee, a slit in the rising benchlands, and wish I were there, alone with the duck pools, alone with the sun and wind and the mushroom shapes the wind had carved out of sandstone.

Older, old enough to fish and hunt on my own, I often went out alone, save for the dog. It was just myself, old Jimps, and fly rod or shotgun, and ahead, personal to me, the bright prospect of game. Later in my life, like my father before me, I turned away from hunting, not liking to kill things anymore. Sometimes, in my sour moments, I almost suspect that grown men who find sport in killing and have their pictures taken with dead deer or elk are cases of arrested adolescence and belong to the National Rifle Association.

At the age of about eleven, when Chick would have been nearly ten, we discovered baseball. It came, that discovery, when we chanced on a book by that great pitcher, Christy Mathewson. It was titled *Pitching in a Pinch,* and we devoured it. We met John McGraw and Josh Devore and Rube Marquard and others and came to fine terms with them. We played catch by the hour, trying this hold and that to make the ball curve.

Choteau had a team then, a team of grown men, and later Chick and I made it, though still adolescents. Of course I had to be the pitcher. Chick, of less standing because of his age, was the catcher. When I went off to college, he became the pitcher and did better than I. He was the superior athlete.

But we didn't go about, Chick and I, as we pleased. We had chores to do. We had to feed and water the chickens and gather the eggs, if any. In winter, with the cow and horse confined, we had to carry water to them and see about oats, middlings, and hay. There were ashes to be taken from the kitchen range and two heaters. We had no central heating and relied on wood and coal. The coal buckets had to be filled and brought in and the wood chopped from blocks that constituted our woodpile. Three kinds of wood were the rule: short kindling for the coal heaters, long kindling and bigger pieces for the kitchen range. Coal was too slow for getting breakfast and supper.

We had no flush toilet in those early days. We made do, like other householders, with a privy and chamber pots under the bed. But we did have running water of a sort. Closed in over one side of the bathroom was a big tank. Over the sink in the kitchen was a force pump. With its nozzle screwed closed, the pump would force water up pipes, through a partition, to the tank. Would force it, that is, if you worked the pump handle. It was my job and Chick's to fill the tank when it went dry. Five hundred strokes it took, each one getting harder than the last until at the end it took all our strength. This task was the more difficult because the kitchen arrangement made it necessary to work the pump with the left hand and arm.

In the shed was a five-gallon container of kerosene, used in our lamps before electricity came, and in the stoves to start fires. Chick or I had to drain it out into smaller containers used in the house. It was a smelly job, made worse by the fact that we always lost the metal cap on the snout and had to jab on a potato as stopper.

We ate well enough by community standards. Flour and sugar came in fifty-pound bags, nothing smaller. What canned goods were available sold for fifteen cents, two for a quarter. When a small storekeeper opened up and introduced pennies into our currency, he won for a first name the somewhat derisive "Penny." Meat was a problem, grass-fed, Texas longhorn, or its crossbreed get. I can still see Mother with a carpenter's hammer pounding away at a steak. For the most part what fruit we had was dried apples, peaches, or apricots, though oranges sometimes came for the Christmas trade and out-of-state travelers took orders for apples, one-fifty a box.

Even so, we lived better than the Blackfoot Indians who camped close to town twice a year. In the fall they were taking their children to the Indian school at Fort Shaw, some thirty miles distant, and in the spring bringing them

A group of young Uinta Ute Indians pose for their photo in the summer of 1909. (Courtesy Special Collections, University of Utah Library)

back to the reservation farther to the north of us. They pitched their tepees on the outskirts and turned their horses out to graze and gave no trouble. But it was not unusual to find one or two of them in an alley, sorting through the garbage for food. And one Sunday at the idled slaughterhouse south of town, I saw a male Indian, eating a length of raw gut. As he chewed and swallowed, he fed it into his mouth with his fingers.

They were starving of course. The buffalo were gone and the promised government rations slow in arrival or inappropriate or inadequate or nonexistent. But as I recall, the town did nothing to help them. My father, who had become the owner and publisher of the Choteau *Acantha,* wrote a sad little piece in which he referred to the survival of the fittest. If greed and slaughter and treachery are the credentials of the fittest, as unhappily they often seem to be, then he was right.

On one occasion, in company with two older girls who carried cameras, I ventured to the encampment. When the girls got to fiddling with their cameras, the Indians put the run on us. They had a thing about having their pictures taken, something to do with the loss of their spirits. The girls were speedier than I in retreat, but I did my best. The Indians—need I say?—meant no harm.

I was a nervous child, as full of anxieties as any psychiatrist could wish. As a young boy I had seen two of my baby sisters die. That made four fatalities, for my parents had buried two in Indiana before I was born. The result was that, at the first signs of illness, I foresaw doom and read it in the sick apprehension in Mother's face. Her dread was mine. It broke me up when, on rare occasions, she let herself cry.

In 1912 Mother took us children to California for the sake of my health and the health of the latest baby, John. In the brood were the baby, Chick and I, and our older sister, Nina Bess, a lovely and loving girl whom we adored. Early that spring in Ontario she died of spinal meningitis, possibly the result of a tick

bite. She was just short of fourteen years old. My father came to California to accompany us home. Five months later Baby John died, they said of bronchitis. There were just two of us left then, two out of eight. Sister Janie came along one year later, when I was thirteen years old.

Over the years Mother's spirit faded. She was always loving-kindness, but the old vivacity was gone. She spoke less, her voice soft and her smile slow, and she didn't sing anymore. It was the deaths that did her in, those and a husband who couldn't or wouldn't control his temper. He was never physical with any one of us, but his words, uttered in that iron voice, were like blows whether addressed to us or provoked by some little mishap or interruption of plan. Almost never did Mother speak up or rebuke him. Open conflict between parents was bad for the children. Sometimes I suspect now that he was indulging himself, enjoying his instant rages, deriving some perverse pleasure out of our unease. But I don't know. I don't know what furies rode him.

And I do not want to be false to his memory. He was capable of great kindness and controlled consideration if any of us felt in deep trouble. He had an active social sense. He sought to improve his community by example and deed. He and Mother gave a sort of tone to a rough town, observing the amenities as they did. He promoted the planting of trees, notably in the cemetery that lay on a bare hill wiry with wild grass, windswept, dug in by gophers. As secretary of the cemetery board—which meant he was it—he ordered ash trees for the burial ground and saw to their planting. For three or four summers, when the saplings were just taking hold, George Jackson, my friend, and I watered them on Saturdays. The outlets were only two, and the hoses heavy canvas, which we had to snake through the headstones and loop over the lot stakes. It took a long day. Once we drowned out a weasel. It came from a gopher hole, wet and savage, and leaped at us. I suppose we killed it but don't remember.

Today the cemetery is shady, sheltered and green, and visitors walk on kept grass to the graves of their loved ones, remarking now and then on old families and the upright tombstones of another day. The improvement owes itself to my father almost entirely.

When Chick came down with scarlet fever and, as a result, could not raise his arms above his shoulders, Father took him to what we called the Old House and stayed with him until his recovery. The reason, of course, was the fear that one of us others would contract the disease. The Old House wasn't a house but a large, rude room at the rear of our lot. It had been there when Father purchased the place. I can see him carrying bedding there, see him morning, noon, and night coming to the house for hot meals for Chickie, and, carefully, trudging back with them on a tray. Fortunately it was summer, and his duties as high school principal were somewhat in suspension. It was a happy day, with Chick well again, when the two came home.

While it existed, Father played the tuba in the Teton County Silver Cornet Band and often practiced at home. When he did, Chick went outside and sat on the back step and cried. Loud noises distressed him. He was a gentle child and outwardly quite placid but suddenly, for no apparent reason, started stuttering and kept it up for a year. A psychiatrist might have explained it. Mother cured it by patience.

We children attended Sunday school while our parents went to morning worship. There was an evening service, too, attended by all of us. Our parents weren't Methodists, but the Methodist church was the only one in town, and they believed in exposure to Christian belief. How far their convictions went, I'm not sure, but they would have upset a fundamentalist. They believed in the ethics of Jesus, but they didn't think he could walk on water or transform a few loaves and fishes into food for the multitude. I know they had some hope of a hereafter, but it was a last-ditch hope. My father once said that without a hereafter, life was a hoax, but I'm sure he had read that somewhere and found little assurance in it. Despite his doubts, he taught the Methodist Bible class for

*Cowboys hard at work branding cattle in
a typical corral. (Courtesy Special Collections,
University of Nevada-Reno Library)*

A sign for a Chinese restaurant (extreme upper right of photo)
competes with banners for busy saloons on the main street of a Utah town.
(Courtesy Utah State Historical Society)

twenty-six years, avoiding the questions of the true believers. For a time he sang in the choir.

Like others in the family, I attended the Choteau grade school and in the beginning liked it hardly as well as the Sunday sessions. I started when I was six years old–plus and attended half a day. On my return I told Mother I didn't like it and didn't want to go back. She smiled and kissed me. Perhaps she was thinking of my health or the fact that I could read already. No matter. Mother was Mother. She said all right. I didn't have to go. And I didn't, not for a whole year. When I did, I found that I liked school, though I never admitted it. Reading was fun. So were spelling and arithmetic, and I floated along, getting top grades. I was always a competitive youngster and enjoyed challenge.

My memories keep returning to the town. It was still frontier in the early 1900s and by broad measure still is, for the West keeps evolving. Frederick Jackson Turner put 1890 as the end of the frontier. If I had to put an arbitrary close to it, I would say it ended with the introduction of the automobile and tractor. Cowpunchers, cowboys if you will, became or gave way to mechanics then, except for those who resorted to rodeo. And the workhorse went out of the picture, together with the teamster, and the working saddle horse didn't work much.

I remember Choteau as a stockmen's town, which in an evolved way it still is. The clank of spurs often sounded on boardwalks. The horse-drawn stagecoach rolled to the hotel in the evening, its whirling iron tires striking sparks from the gravel. Now and then a string of horned cattle trailed through the place, messing the streets, bawling as they went. The stagecoach and freight wagon served the town. The streets were made wide so that a teamster with several yoke of draft animals, pulling two or more wagons, could turn around without trouble.

Saloons outnumbered the churches, three to one, and Eva Fox's whorehouse, not called that in public, sat kitty-corner down from the Beaupre House.

Seeing men go in there, I wondered, though I knew hardly a thing about sex. My parents were starchy. They avoided the subject except, when circumstances demanded comment, they used the word *nasty*. I wonder sometimes that they brought nine children into the world.

There were the stagecoach to watch and the freight wagons and Eva Fox's to cast a covert glance at, and old Soo Son's, the Chinaman's restaurant, curtained inside so that decent people couldn't see the sinful women and be contaminated by the sight. There were these things and more, and always the great outdoors.

These experiences, impressions, and boyish observations went into my making, I suppose—they and others here overlooked and still others that came after. I think space has shaped me, space and distance and the outdoors, the great outdoors and the free. It pleases me, as it did in those young years, to see buttes rising in the shimmered heat, to know the lasting promise of mountains and from them get my directions, to be able to identify the flowers that freshen spring and the animals that share my occupation of the universe.

What I've written is of long years ago, but somehow, as someone has said of his childhood, it all was just yesterday.

DAVID LAVENDER

David Lavender has just the kind of background you would wish for a Western writer. Born in the still-booming gold-and-silver-mining town of Telluride, Colorado, in 1910, Lavender's early years were filled with the kind of images and experiences people have come to associate with the West—the mythological West, with the enormous peaks and crags of mountain ranges being turned inside out for their precious ores, and the rugged valleys alive with dusty, milling cattle on the long drive to market. He was raised in the kind of landscape that you see anymore only in old big-budget Hollywood Westerns on late-night TV. And he's tried, throughout his writing career and his life, to keep some of that spirit alive in himself.

He lives now in Ojai, California, in semi-arid citrus-and-ranch country outside Los Angeles. His home of more than forty-five years lies at the base of the Topa Topa Mountains, hardly a stone's throw from Thacher School, a private school where he was head of the English department until 1970. "As long as you have to live in California, this is a good place," he admits, although he hasn't lost his love of Colorado, and returns to the Rockies every summer to visit his son David living near Telluride and take in the sights of his home ground.

Look at Lavender's early years and you'll see why the career of Western writer seems so right for him. Born in Telluride while the mining industry was still going full steam, he grew up in the midst of boomtown chaos and soaked up the excitement of the mining life, including the dangers, when a flooded creek jumped its banks in a thunderstorm and nearly succeeded in burying the town in mud. A short time after that, at age six, Lavender's parents separated, and he found himself for a time in Denver with his mother and younger brother, Dwight. When they returned to Telluride six years later, Lavender had a new stepfather and an opportunity to work on his cattle ranch.

Edgar Lavender was a successful freight operator in Telluride who ran goods up to the mines by wagon and pack mule. When his business was squeezed out by automation (aerial trams replaced the need for wagon routes), he took up ranching, operating in the hills and valleys near the San Miguel River. Here Lavender learned from his stepfather, working the ranch for more than ten years, ranging around the Southwest from Telluride down to the areas that now make up Canyonlands National Park and back.

He took a break for a time to "go back East and learn how to wear shoes," as he puts it, completing high school in Pennsylvania, with the intent of going to Harvard and becoming a lawyer. He instead received a degree from Princeton, in 1931, and went on to a year of graduate study in law at Stanford University before being called back by his stepfather to help him keep the ranch operating as the Depression began to set in. He worked there until Ed Lavender died of stomach cancer in 1934, leaving him to keep the operation afloat as long as he could. When the ranch finally went bust, Lavender took his first wife, Martha, and son to Denver, where he worked for a short time in an advertising agency. It was at that point that he finally decided on a change of scene, packing up and moving to California in 1938.

"I wanted to clear out the cobwebs and start over again," he told me, and it was at this point that he began to think of becoming a writer. He spent about eighteen months in Los Angeles ("And hated it," he confessed) before he was offered a teaching job at the Thacher School in Ojai. Taking over for a young

*David Lavender visits
the riding arena at
Thacher School in
Ojai, California.
(Photo by Joe Backes)*

English teacher who had been drafted for World War II, Lavender enjoyed the job so much that he decided to stay. He alternated his teaching time with writing, continuing the love for research he had discovered at college.

"It was a natural thing to turn to, I guess, and I had to turn to something. Without that to fall back on I don't know what I would have done." His first major project was an autobiography of sorts, a collection of thoughts and perceptions on a land that he hadn't entirely left behind. *One Man's West,* published by Doubleday in 1943, was a fascinating account of the mining and ranching industries as seen from the perspective of someone who had been there, and the book was well received by critics and readers alike.

Although critics have often praised his work for the accuracy of his facts and the amount of research he does for each piece, Lavender really does not see himself as a historian but rather as a writer who writes about history because it's interesting. He tries to remain true to the spirit of the West in his work, and the love he has for the land he was raised in. Some of his better-known works—including *Bent's Fort* (Doubleday, 1954), about the famous trading post lying on the Arkansas River in Colorado, *The Fist in the Wilderness* (Doubleday, 1964), the history of the American Fur Company, and *The Great Persuader* (Doubleday, 1970), the story of rail baron Collis P. Huntington and the construction of the Central Pacific Railroad—try in their detail and scope to capture some of that spirit. And it's obvious he's succeeded, given the number of awards and honors bestowed upon him by such organizations as the Western Writers of America (for *Bent's Fort*), the Cowboy Hall of Fame (for the *Great West*), the American Association for State and Local History (for *The Rockies* in 1968), and the California Historical Society's Award of Merit in 1980 for Lavender's outstanding contributions to California history. Even the few times he's written fiction, including *Andy Claybourne* in 1946 and *Red Mountain* in 1963 (both published by Doubleday), he's drawn on his own experiences in ranching and mining for accuracy.

*David Lavender
at home. (Photo
by Joe Backes)*

It's that sense of maintaining the spirit of the land that is most important to Lavender, being true to the past and letting it speak for itself. In *Old Southwest, New Southwest: Essays on a Region and Its Literature,* published through the University of Arizona Press in 1987 for the Writers of the Purple Sage Project conference on southwestern literature, Lavender's essay "The Tyranny of Facts" tries to prove just that. He mentions how in historical fiction many writers cloud the identities of historic places and people by changing their names, in order then to bend the events to fit the narrative. He gives many examples, including one of his own works, the mining novel *Red Mountain,* in which the town of Ouray, Colorado (where Lavender himself worked for a time in the Camp Bird Mine), became the town of Argent.

"These changes don't fool anyone," he wrote, "but they do serve as a kind of mumbo-jumbo to hold carping critics at bay. If one complains about errors of fact, the author need only say, 'I wasn't writing about Ouray and its early day rambunctious characters. I was writing about places and people similar to them, so go away and let me handle the drama as my narrative demands—a narrative which, after all, has its own kind of truth.'"

He went on to explain to me: "The borderline between fiction and fact is always pretty slippery. I have to be on the side of believing if you can't get your drama out of what really happened, you better look to something else for your story."

It seems as if sticking to that truth in his career has worked well for Lavender: twenty-five books written over the course of forty-five years, many considered landmarks in the field of Western history; his work as a consultant to the library at the University of California at Santa Barbara since 1982; his membership in the American Society of Historians and service on the board of directors of the Southwest National Parks and Monuments Association; teacher, environmentalist, and outdoorsman—all seem so appropriate for this man born and raised among the dramatic ranges of the southern Rockies.

I asked him, as our conversation was winding down, if he thought things might be different had the ranch not failed. Would he still be out there, riding the range and leading the cattle up and down the valleys and hills?

"That's a good question," he responded, chuckling, knowing more than I did the pull that the land still has on him. "Certainly there's a great deal about it that I love, but the perils and the heartbreak and the narrow horizons would have eventually gotten me down. I think I'm lucky I got thrown out when I did. It held no cultural advantages at all, something I had a taste of back East and don't think I could have gotten along without."

But the West is inbred in Lavender now, and he's in no hurry to escape it. He's remaining true to his roots, honest about where he's going and where he's been. His time now is spent writing (currently working on a project on the Nez Percé tribe), walking, or horseback riding when he can, visiting with the faculty and students at Thacher School. On the whole he is content, possessing the kind of quiet calm you get from staying in touch with the land. As he wrote to *Contemporary Authors* for their write-up on his career:

"This job of mine could hardly be better. I explore the best parts of the American West—backpacking, riding horseback, and sometimes in jeeps or rafting, in order to acquire for my writing a sense of immediacy and reality. Then as I read what others have said on the subject and as I refine my own thoughts during the process of writing, a new sort of energizing takes over and I find myself looking with new eyes and a new understanding at old scenes, a constant sequence of rediscoveries, as it were. No, I don't get tired of the West; it is too big and too dynamic, and filled with too many choice inhabitants."

You really can't say it any better than that.

M.B., 1989

A family home shares a hillside with a large mining operation in Telluride, Colorado. (Courtesy Western Historical Collection, University of Colorado, Boulder)

Bonanza Land

The San Juan Mountain uplift in southwestern Colorado was, during my childhood, strong on visual drama but short on cultural resources. The latter I picked up, bits and pieces, in the East during two years of high school and four of college. Somehow, though, I never did get around to writing about the East.

Consider. Telluride, Colorado, where I was born in 1910, sits near the closed end of a profound U-shaped glacial trough, gathering place for the San Miguel River. The peaks rising along the rim of that giant horseshoe hit the sky at from thirteen thousand to fourteen thousand feet above sea level. From that beginning the land falls northwest through a sequence of marvelously varied ecological zones: cool, dark forests of spruce and fir; lush grazing grounds on aspen-covered mesas; to sagebrush flats girt with stately belts of ponderosa pine; gnarled mazes of piñons and blue-berried junipers; and finally, near the Utah border, cliff-lined valleys and canyons whose gritty red soil is enhanced by vivid green fields of irrigated alfalfa.

The swath we followed through this country, back and forth with the seasons, was about seventy-five miles long and roughly parallel to the San Miguel River. Relatively few people lived in the area. They were knowledgeable in their way. All, females included, understood how to castrate calves. Most had eaten the takings, called Rocky Mountain oysters, after the juicy lumps had been broiled on rusty grills extemporized from branding irons. None of them—here I am not counting visitors from the outside—had ever heard, or heard of, Verdi's *Requiem*. Although they were intimate with the land, the name Thoreau was missing from their vocabularies. Art was what graced the calendars that garage mechanics, redolent of lubricating grease, hung on the walls of the littered cubicles where they made out their bills with the blunt tips of grubby pencil stubs.

However.

The same glacial ice that had scoured out the upper canyon of the San Miguel River, where Telluride crouches, had carved the surrounding peaks into spectacular horns, spires, saw-toothed arêtes, and heavy-shouldered humps buttressed by ridges of weather-shattered rock. The melting of the snowpack each spring shows this high country to be as gray, mostly, as the hide of a hippopotamus, for the capping of the San Juan bulge is made up of what's left of massive layers of congealed lavas, breccias, and tuffs. The material was laid down some thirty million years ago, give or take a few million either way, by several intermittently bellowing volcanoes. At least twenty of those huge, dead vents have been identified by geologists. Because the geologists worked easily among the local people and because miners are naturally interested in rocks, a lot of their earth knowledge trickled down to the rest of us. Probably our gleanings were more superficial than we realized. Just the same, you absorb, in such informal classrooms, a sense of wonder about the vast sweep of time and the Earth that requiems miss, majestic though some of them are.

Other bits of earth knowledge enlivened the tales we heard from our elders. Here and there the high gray ridges and cirques above timberline (about eleven thousand feet elevation in the San Juan Mountains) are splotched and streaked with bright reds, oranges, and yellows. Prospectors had learned long since that such stains are the spoor of hot mineral juices welling up, through fissures, from the earth's molten interior. In places those juices,

A formally attired group picks poppies at the foot of a California mountain at the turn of the century. (Seaver Center, Natural History Museum of Los Angeles County)

solidifying underground into ore, contain significant amounts of gold, silver, copper, lead, and zinc. A natural resource, in short. And untrammeled access to fortuitous natural resources has been, for much too long a time, what the West is all about.

In the mid-1870s, so our Homers sang, adventuresome prospectors had first sighted those colored stains on the gray uplands. They had also found sprinkles of placer gold in riverside gravels that had been washed out of the high country by a million years of grinding snowmelt. Such discoveries drew into the area an accelerating flow of eager exploiters. Charles Painter, my grandfather-to-be, was one of them. So were Sievert Rowher (my middle name is Sievert), his wife Eliese, a grown son, George, and a daughter named for her mother—Eliese Catherine. There may have been more Rowhers along; I haven't been able to learn.

Political trouble of some sort had caused the Rowhers to emigrate, shortly after our Civil War, from the Danish part of Schleswig-Holstein to Springfield, Missouri, in the Ozark Mountains. There they found, in addition to herds of dairy cows reminiscent of Denmark, several busy lead and zinc mines. Association with those mines, whether as laborers or bookkeepers I don't know, may be what led Sievert and George Rowher to reflect on the desirability of finding a mine of their own. Hearing of the San Juans, off the family went. They may have bought railroad tickets for the first part of the journey. The last part, where tracks had not yet been laid, they crossed in a wagon roofed with canvas to shelter their household goods from the hard-clanging summer thunderstorms of the southern Rockies.

There were few unattached women in Telluride in those days. Charles Painter, recently arrived from Ohio, met Eliese Catherine Rowher almost as soon as she appeared. They were married in 1882—a vintage year. Charles had just been elected mayor of the town. (He was already clerk of San Miguel County.) She was twenty-one; he, twenty-six. Their first child, another George,

Yosemite Falls provides a spectacular backdrop for a walk along the Old Road in 1910. (Seaver Center, Natural History Museum of Los Angeles)

Three workmen pose beside their small rail car, used to repair and maintain the mine tracks. Early 1900s. (Courtesy Western Historical Collection, University of Colorado, Boulder)

was born ten months later. Random atoms coalescing into energetic nuclei: Such mixings of bloodlines and nationalities were a feature of the mining camps of the American West.

By the time of his marriage, Charlie Painter had learned that working underground was not the quickest way to prosperity. Somehow he got hold of the struggling Telluride *Journal.* To it he added a title-and-abstract business—a necessary calling in a land where mining claims overlapped like a deck of messed-up cards. The wisdom of his choices was soon reflected in the house he and Eliese built. Bonanza Victorian, many-gabled, lavishly curlicued, and painted gray edged with white, it echoed the gabled peaks of the surrounding mountains. For myself, I recall the plumbing best: an enormous claw-footed, zinc-lined bathtub in which my brother, Dwight, fifteen months younger, and I played happily for hours with our rubber ducks and steamboats. And the toilet. Its walnut tank stood way up by the ceiling and was activated by a chain dangling within reach of the user.

The lot fitted the house. Most building sites in mining camps are long but narrow in order to make maximum use of the limited amounts of ground available for home and business construction. But Granddad ignored the crowded pattern. He erected his gables on a corner lot, double-sized, on the high side of the street—no blocked views for him. The house was smack in the center of town, one block *up* the south-facing slope from the town's main street.

Up was important. The south-facing slope of the canyon caught the few hours of winter sunlight that slipped over the top of the much steeper, heavily timbered hill on the other side of the canyon. The San Miguel River runs along that hill's base. Its banks gave ingress to the little narrow-gauge railroad, now extinct, that was welcomed into the box canyon in November 1890 by the vigorous tootlings of the Telluride cornet band and by blasts of giant powder that rolled like thunder between the canyon's constricting walls. The depot was *down* there, three blocks below Main Street. So were the freight yards, the warehouses of the Telluride Transfer Company, and the many livery stables with their humming swarms of flies. That was where the Finn-Swede Hall was located, along with the homes of many of the foreign-born laborers. Also it was the site of dance halls and saloons and the tightly packed rows of cribs where a constantly shifting cast of soiled doves plied their trade. No Telluride boy, even if he didn't become a customer, ever needed to sit at Daddy's knee for an introductory lecture about life's sometimes forbidden fruits.

At the turn of the century the town's social and physical cleavages grew bloody. The intensely radical Western Federation of Miners swept into Colorado after an alarming career in Idaho and Montana. To advertise its potency, the Telluride local bought a building site smack-dab in the middle of the elite sunny side of town and there erected, to the astonished displeasure of the stiff-collared residents, the Miners' Union meeting hall and hospital. Simultaneously labor strife erupted. The superintendent of the big Smuggler-Union Mine was assassinated. (The word "Union" in that context was the name of one of the conglomerated early mines and in no way referred to labor organizations.) Unionized workers fought a day-long gun battle with scabs far up the hill at the mouth of the Smuggler-Union's prosperous Bullion Tunnel. It ended with the scabs being driven out of the region across Imogene Pass, 13,100 feet high. The little fort that was built of talus rocks to keep them from returning to Telluride, where many of them had families, can still be seen frowning down on the jeep road to Ouray.

Local businessmen, Charlie Painter in the lead, formed a Citizens Alliance to support the mine owners. When the state militia arrived in the fall of 1904 to restore order, units of the alliance were sworn in as volunteers. Granddad supervised the passing out of rifles to them—he recorded names and serial numbers—and at the pep meeting that followed he delivered, as his answer to the union's talk of "industrial slavery," an impassioned speech about the sanctity of property and the Christian duty of every mine superintendent to produce worthy returns for his stockholders. Insofar as the turmoil produced a victor, it was the mine owners and the Citizens Alliance.

Memories of the antagonisms and of the problems it created for my own birthing troubled me as I grew aware of them. That's part of the reason for writing this account of things that occurred before my appearance. Memory is not just a matter of direct recollection. It also springs from tales read or heard and then hoarded in a family's or community's sense of itself. And what I heard and read (or what I think I heard and read) of my grandfather in no way jibes with my direct recollections of him.

He and Eliese had four children, two boys and two girls. My father, David, the second son, went outside, to Denver University, to complete his education. There he met Edith Garrigues, daughter of a justice of the Supreme Court of Colorado, and brought her back to Telluride as a bride. He supported her by working on his father's newspaper.

His brother and sisters and their children also lived in Telluride. With this often obstreperous collection of descendants, Granddad, as we called him, was unfailingly gentle, playful, and patient. During later life he became clean shaven, but he still appears to me in a precisely trimmed, pointed Vandyke beard and mustache, grown as if to keep step with his gabled house. He was of medium height and somewhat paunchy. His wife—I never knew of them to quarrel—cut her prematurely gray hair fairly short and wore it in a tight bun on the top of her head. Perhaps because she was slightly deaf, her voice became loud and high-pitched. She had one of the heartiest laughs I ever heard. She fed us enormous helpings of German and Danish pastries and calmed us as we struggled for first right to lick the dasher of the ice-cream freezer—all in her big kitchen. We were in awe of the formal dining room with its glass-fronted cabinets filled with rows of painted china and of the living room with its lace net curtains, heavy draperies, and Tiffany lamps. But how

Snow piled in the middle of downtown Telluride in the early 1920s. (David Lavender family collection)

we loved to roll on the big, slanting lawn, outside the front-room windows, scarcely noticing, except subconsciously, the great peaks crowning the hillsides.

By the time Mother's first accouchement arrived, the handing out of the rifles during the strike was six years past. But, so the tale runs, my gentle, playful grandfather had not forgotten the intensities of the mountain warfare. He refused to let me be born in the Miners' Union hospital, though the existence of a hospital in so raw a place was said to be one of the reasons Mother had been willing to move to Telluride.

I suppose there were rows about this. But, after all, home deliveries were common in those days. The double bed in our own narrow little house was again taken apart so it could be carried down the steep stairs and reassembled close to the living room's bulbous black heating stove, bright with trimmings of polished steel. Dr. Hadley, who took care of the sunny side of town, arrived by buggy at the beginning of the frigid night of February 4—he had a car, the wonder of the camp, but it couldn't handle the snow—and that was that, as far as I was concerned. It was that, as well, when my brother, Dwight, was born. The home deliveries didn't hurt us, of course, but I have pondered the story at times, for it could not have happened quite as described. The Miners' Union hospital perished during the labor strife and was not operating at the time of my and my brother's birth. Another hospital was in business, however. Why weren't we born there? I have no idea. The reason is lost, buried under the cinders of ancient acrimonies. But somewhere along the way the acids penetrated the folk tales of our family. The Miners' Union hospital lived on in memory just to be hated—another version of the old chestnut about feuds continuing after the cause has disappeared.

My few more accurate images of my early years in Telluride are like the flickerings of a disorganized slide show. I have kaleidoscopic impressions of Mother returning from our summer picnics with the color high in her cheeks—

she was a very beautiful woman—and her arms filled with blue-and-white columbines and ivory-white mariposa lilies, their centers as radiant as rainbows. In winter we were bundled up as round as balls and dragged about on Flexible Flyer sleds. Occasionally, as we grew older, we were allowed to squeeze into the middle of a single-file crowd of tobogganers and go lickety-split, whooping and laughing in exhilaration, down one of the side streets that the town council had closed to other traffic.

The summer I was four was unusually rainy. The creeks were high and turbid—especially Cornet Creek, which leaped over a sixty-foot waterfall at the upper edge of town. To gain room for more lots, developers had turned the creek's water into an artificial channel that curved away from the land they wanted. It was a mistake.

Cornet Creek takes form in a big basin under the stone prickles that crown Santa Sophia Ridge—old-timers called it Sawtooth Mountain. The workings of the Liberty Bell Mine sprawled across the lower end of the basin. Clearly this was avalanche country; the mine company had erected protective barriers. Inadequate ones. In 1902 a monstrous slide killed Grandmother's brother, George Rowher, and eighteen others. My stepfather-to-be was lucky to get away with a severe pummeling. In the summer of 1914, an afternoon cloudburst hit the basin. A wall of water demolished the Liberty Bell's waste dump—the powdery gray mill tailings turned the howling flood into syrup—and then whammed into Cornet Canyon. There it gathered up a freight of giant boulders and down timber that had been accumulating for years.

An office worker at the Liberty Bell telephoned a warning to the town. I suppose the bell in the tower of the firehouse began a frenzied clanging, but I did not hear it. Nor did I see housewives running about either screaming for their children, out playing, or rushing them to safety. My brother and I were in the kitchen. Suddenly Mother, pale with terror, stooped to lay hold of us and then froze, an arm around each of us for I have no idea how long.

*A group of children sled across streetcar tracks in
Salt Lake City as parents and a local police officer
look on. (Courtesy Utah State Historical Society)*

A washday afternoon in Bingham Canyon, Utah. The ore car above is bringing coal from a nearby mine. (Courtesy Utah State Historical Society)

The creek had jumped its artificial channel and was seeking its old path. But that egress had been filled and built on. Unrestrained, the torrent spread wildly, without pattern, a thick, scallop-edged, boulder-filled, fast-rushing goo. The din, as I remember it—or as I remember being told about it—was paralyzing.

As the noise diminished, we emerged from our cave of fear. But then I grew even more afraid. Until the rain had started, I had been out there in what was to me the permanent order of my life, a geometric pattern of neatly arranged houses, many of them sheltering children of Dwight's and my age. Now everything was chaos. Though our home and a few others had somehow escaped serious damage, others had been less fortunate. Two or three had been crushed. A few others had been pushed, weirdly canting, off their narrow lots into the streets. Many had been twisted off their foundations. One huge boulder, taller than I, had snuggled up against Granddad's coal shed without cracking a board; their house, several blocks from ours, had also escaped. But the lobby of the Sheridan Hotel, on the main street, had been filled with mud to within a foot of its ceiling. The nearby thoroughfares were knee-deep swamps of a semiliquid ooze punctuated with grotesque sculptures of tangled debris. The only fatality (I believe) was a woman who was jammed against a house wall and smothered in mud.

I don't remember much about the cleanup. Somehow it happened; squads of volunteers wielding high-pressure fire hoses washed the muck down through the lower part of town into the river. Boulders too big to move (there were no bulldozers then) were dynamited into smaller pieces. Expert blasters from one of the mines broke up the massive rock beside our grandparents' coal shed with no more damage than a few cracked boards—a manifestation of professional skill I did not appreciate until I went to work, many years later, as a common laborer at the fabled Camp Bird Mine, across Imogene Pass from Telluride.

Two years after the flood, the order of our lives was shattered again. My parents separated, and the next six years were years of exile, mostly in Denver.

But you can go home again—sort of. In January 1921 our mother married Ed (for Edgar) Lavender. He gave his name to Dwight and me as well as to her. We may have seen him first, as she did, in Telluride. He had come there from a farm in South Dakota before he was twenty. Gradually he had built up a profitable freighting business using strings of pack mules and two or three big wagons pulled by elegant draft horses, but after the mines began installing aerial tramways for transporting all but their most bulky items, he had turned to land and cattle. His animals ranged along the swath of country mentioned at the beginning of this account. The mountain part of the belt, we were assured, was no great distance from Telluride. The town, moreover, was the county seat. Ed went there now and then on business, and we could go along. Although our father had moved away, our grandparents were still in their gray, gabled house, as welcoming as ever.

All this was comforting. Still, there were many adjustments to make, many new things to learn.

My memory cannot separate our first trip to the ranch from those that followed, all intense with anticipation. The time was late May, which was as early as we could escape from the schools we continued going to in Denver. As the car lurched slowly along the rutted dirt road leading south from our post office town of Norwood, Ed would invariably break his customary silence to remark on the progress of the new grass under the tangled boughs of the scrub oak we passed. But the beacon that gripped Dwight and me was a splendidly isolated peak, still glistening with most of its winter mantle of snow. Shaped like an inverted ice-cream cone, it was 12,613 feet high. In 1874, William Marshall, an early-day surveyor, had written, "It is the most beautiful peak I have ever seen. It is entirely detached from the other mountains, and rises, a solitary, graceful peak, 3,000 feet above its base." The Lone Cone, westernmost summit of the Colorado Rockies. In my opinion, Marshall understated matters.

The principal summer camp of the Pitchfork Ranch, as the outfit was called, sat near the base of the Cone's northwest flank, in a crook formed by a foothill ridge that ran west for a ways and then bent northwest. The ranch name derived from the replica of a three-tined pitchfork that was burned with a hot iron onto the sides of Ed's cows and steers and, more neatly, onto the hips of the horses. Further identification came from cropping the cattle's ears midway, a procedure that sped recognition of our animals in a crowded herd where brands were not readily visible.

The foothill ridge, steep-sided, broad-topped, and brushy, blocked our view to the west. But, as we had been promised, we could see, some thirty miles to the east (fifty-five miles by car) the mountains that lined the San Miguel River below Telluride. Space flowed in from the north. A tremendous vista: gray-yellow sagebrush flats, black, far-off reaches of pine and juniper, and, on the horizon, dimmed by distance, the flat line of the Uncompahgre Plateau.

The habitations tucked into the crook of the foothill ridge were, by the standards of southwestern Colorado, ancient. Ed had purchased the buildings and land piece by piece—some two thousand acres of land, altogether—from the last of a long sequence of owners. The different shades of gray in the rail fences of the corrals indicated repeated patching. The thick ponderosa pine logs of the barn (we called them yellow pine) and the hand-driven shakes of the roof were decaying. The upright planks of pine that sheathed the main house were weathered to beautiful tones of tan and brown. But at least Ed's marriage had brought it a new roof.

Inside the house were three comfortably big rooms that opened into each other like the cars of a train. Other doors led from each room onto the porch, which was shaded and left viewless the last part of each summer by a mass of self-renewing, fast-growing hop vines. Closest to the barn was Mother and Ed's combined sitting and bedroom, warmed by a fine fireplace and decorated with bear and coyote skins and several soft-hued Navajo rugs. The dining room embraced a huge table covered with oilcloth; there enormous meals were served three times a day to whoever was on the place at the time. One wall sported an oil painting of a dead magpie lying on its back, feet up in the air. I cannot imagine why the artist, a Telluride woman, chose that subject, but she occasionally paid unannounced visits, and it had to stay. A ravenous wood-burning stove, water heater attached, dominated the kitchen. The cook's room was a lean-to at the west end of the structure.

Outliers were the bunkhouse, with its four iron bedsteads; the storehouse, where groceries bought in wholesale lots were stored and binned; and the wooden-floored, half-walled tents where Dwight and I slept with the ranch's two black-and-white pointers. Add a chicken coop, a milk house with its various troughs and shelves, a screened meat house, where beef was hung when the weather was cool enough for butchering, and the privy. And the root cellar. Late each summer, after potatoes had matured in the low country, Ed brought up more than we could use that fall. By spring they were exuding long, pale, crooked sprouts, and were softening. It was Dwight's and my job to break off the pallid sprouts and toss whatever potatoes were unusable over the fence to the milk cows. Watching their faces as they tried to chew more than their mouths could readily hold was the only recompense for the chore.

Once this little settlement had drawn its water from a deep, hand-dug, stone-lined well into which various small creatures fell and were drowned. Shortly before Dwight's and my arrival it was abandoned in favor of water from an easier, cleaner source—a smallish irrigation canal that curved like a snake along the base of the foothill range on its way to a vaguely cooperative agricultural community halfway between the mountains and the desert. Because the canal crossed a corner of his property and blocked a couple of tiny streams, Ed obtained the right to tap it with a little ditch that leaped cheerily down among scattered pines to a wooden basin just back of the kitchen. There we dipped up in buckets the water needed in the kitchen and on the flower beds. We then ran the stream through the milk house, and when rains were deficient Ed used the flow for irrigating his vegetable patch with its trellised peas and bulging heads of lettuce and cabbage.

The unused water slid down a small hill into a slough. Ed put an earth dam across the slough about a quarter of a mile from the house. This created a pond where stock could drink—and where Ed could hunt ducks. Dwight and I used it for a swimming hole. We built a tipsy raft and later, stripped naked, took our horses in. Some swam straightaway, nostrils lifted just above the ripples. It was

Ed Lavender displays the day's hunt. These grouse (he called them prairie chickens) were bagged at the summer camp in the mid-1920s. (David Lavender family collection)

more fun to find one that panicked, reached for the ground, leaped up, and sank again. Up down, up down, until finally it got beyond its depth and *had* to swim. We learned to swim about the same way. No one taught us; we just thrashed clumsily along.

While absorbing all this, Dwight and I also had to get acquainted with Ed. He wasn't much help. A taciturn, longtime bachelor, he knew nothing about getting along with partly grown children. But in his way he tried. He demonstrated, mostly in silence, how to catch and saddle a horse and how to handle a .22 rifle and a 410-gauge shotgun. It wasn't his fault that one afternoon while a cousin and I were shooting at targets with my beloved lever-action .22 I got hit in the foot. After gangrene had set in, I landed in the hospital in Telluride. A close call. But at least I had learned always to put a loaded gun on safety catch.

Getting shot in the foot is, of course, a standard metaphor for ineptitude. Ed never turned the episode into a lesson, however. He treated it as he might a break in the irrigation ditch. Such things happened; you fixed them and went on. The reaction (I know now it shouldn't have seemed so unexpected) helped Dwight and me get over being so wary of him. I think it also eased his wariness of us. Anyway, as we grew older and began riding silently around the summer camp with Ed, meeting the kind of troubles that animals perversely land themselves in, we achieved a kind of reciprocity I still can't quite define. Affection? Well, yes, though never overt. Respect, certainly.

Ed was of medium height and deeply tanned. His mustache was clipped off at the corners of his mouth; his thick hair, but not that dark mustache, slowly turned iron gray. He had a countywide reputation—perhaps statewide, to judge from what I heard later from his fellow members at the Denver Club—as a bridge and poker player. His only other recreation, aside from going to the bunkhouse to listen to the cowboys yarn, was hunting game birds. He was deadly accurate with his double-barreled Parker shotguns. I never saw him touch a pistol.

He assigned my brother and me what seemed to us, during our first summers at the ranch, a long list of duties. We kept the woodbox in the kitchen full of aspen chunks. We lugged water to the flower beds that at Mother's insistence we helped clear out of the weeds inside the fenced yard. We fed chickens morning and night and were careful, supposedly, to shut out coyotes and foxes by always closing the door of the coop just before dark. Cleaning that coop once each summer was as unpleasant as handling rotted potatoes. At evening we hurried the cows, their heavy udders swinging, back to the calves in their pens so that the ranch handyman could finish the milking in good time. More exciting, after we had learned to stay atop our mounts, was taking turns at saddling up the night horse and galloping out through the cool sunrise to bring in the geldings and mares that would be needed for the day.

Shortly after we were settled at the summer camp, the slow-plodding cattle began dribbling in, shoved along by tired cowboys. The first to arrive were cows that had wintered on the hay farms in Paradox Valley seventy miles away, where their calves had been born only eight or ten weeks before. (The chromatic, flat-bottomed, cliff-walled, largely arid valley was called Paradox because the Dolores River, on its way to pick up the San Miguel, flowed across rather than along it.) As soon as the herd arrived, a frenzy of branding began— smoky fires, swirling ropes, exasperated oaths, the stink of burned hair and of cowpies inadvertently sat in when one of the men wrestled a terrified calf to the ground. Until we grew bigger, Dwight and I tallied the number branded— each heifer, each steer, and, on rare occasions, a bull calf of notable-enough lines that Ed decided to leave it uncastrated.

The branding finished, the animals were scattered out in nearby pastures, some leased, until they were driven back to what we hoped would be a mild winter in Paradox and its surrounding breaks. At that point I learned from Ed a fine, two-bit word: *transhumance,* the movement of herds to different grazing grounds as the seasons change. As for the cowboys, they were as true nomads as were the wanderers of the Sudan or of the steppes of central Asia.

Only the calving cows had luxuriated in the feedlots of Paradox. Stronger animals—yearling steers, which was what urban meat eaters wanted most, dry cows, and a few whose pregnancy had escaped notice—rustled for themselves. The names of the places where they ranged had a wonderful ring—Wild Steer Mesa on one side of Paradox, Saucer Basin on the other. Sinbad, Roc Creek (note the spelling), Long Draw, Bull Canyon, Dry Creek, Big Gyp, for gypsum. They were places of crumpled sandstone, slit canyons, precipitous rimrock, hidden springs, gnats, twisted trees, and sudden openings that looked out over heart-stopping vistas.

While we were tending the cows and calves at the summer camp, roundup crews were sweeping those formidable breaks. That done, the riders started slowly upcountry with their gleanings, meanwhile searching the sage-and-piñon flats and the oak-brush mesas for other animals that were already following, as instinctively as deer, the new grass sprouting in the foothills.

The gatherings were driven onto preassigned bunch grounds. There representatives of the different outfits in our seventy-mile neighborhood saddled up their nimblest, best-trained cutting horses and rode into the herd to find and chivy out into separate bunches whatever animals wore their ranch's brand. There were lightninglike maneuvers and occasional falls under choking clouds of dust, ringing oaths, and great pride in good horses.

Each year the final bunch ground was on one of the flats near the Lone Cone. Dwight's and my initial roundup assignment was to help hold the Pitchfork bunch together. We didn't do much more at first than occupy space. But I know now that we were fortunate to be there at all. The open range—"our" range, we said, although it was public domain that we used, free of charge—was disappearing under the onslaught of World War I veterans taking advantage of liberalized homesteading laws. Some of the nesters were served by the irrigation canal that flowed past the summer camp. Even with that water, few

Cowboys work to get the upper hand over a reluctant horse.
(Courtesy Special Collections, University of Nevada-Reno Library)

David Lavender, age twelve (on the far left), "keeping tally of cattle branded." Around 1922. (David Lavender family collection)

of them could make a go of their desperate work. But in the process of failing they fenced the land into so many plots that it was impossible to turn cattle loose on it and expect them to survive any better than the homesteaders did.

The areawide roundups disappeared with the open range. Our region's final gathering, held again at the foot of the Lone Cone, took place during the summer of 1925. It was, I am reasonably sure, one of the last big, multioutfit roundups in the United States. After that we worked pretty much on our own, driving the cows and calves up from the low country along steppingstones of pastures, some belonging to the Pitchfork and some rented from the home-steaders. (Now the migrant herds are trucked.) We cleaned the breaks by means of greasy-sack rides. The term meant that we carried flour sacks filled with bacon and other food on a couple of packhorses, along with our bedrolls, so we could camp at whatever of those hidden springs suited our convenience. No more chuck wagons. And especially no more chuck wagon cooks. The sweep and excitement of the old days were gone. Or so the cowboys lamented. I thought our rides were fine. That was because I didn't know better. Or so they told me.

We moved the cows and calves and yearling heifers into their summer pastures as usual, and then took the little steers to the east side of the Cone, to a place called Beaver Park. There we turned them loose, under government permit, on Forest Service land they must have thought was heaven. As I did. Beaver Park—it was a huge tilted basin between the Cone and the higher, bulkier Dolores Peaks. Forests freckled with meadows and transected by glit-tering trout streams. Bunchgrass knee-high, vast spangles of wildflowers, with a peaked-roofed cabin as our second summer camp. In the fall we drove the fatted yearlings to Placerville, fifteen miles below Telluride, and shipped them by narrow-gauge railroad to market in Denver. (Paradise lost.) The cows, calves, and growing heifers went back to the low country to begin another round of production.

It was not an efficient way to grow food, and it depended for success on various forms of government bounty. But the foothills of southwestern Colorado were bonanza land for a while, just as the mines above Telluride had been. Cattle prices were high in the mid-1920s. To take advantage of that and also to replace cow-and-calf rangeland lost to the homesteaders, Ed and an associate bought, in 1927, what was called the Club Ranch, after a brand shaped like a club in a deck of cards.

Its winter camp sat on a low bench beside the murky San Miguel River; its summer camp, our third one, was on the brushy top of the Uncompahgre Plateau. We could integrate operations with the Pitchfork unit by driving cattle back and forth between Paradox and the Club winter camp through the spectacular canyon of the Dolores River, just above its junction with the San Miguel. It was a hair-raising trail, particularly when slick with ice. Later, after the huge uranium-milling complex called Uravan had taken over the Club winter camp (it produced most of the uranium used in the first atom bomb), the company built a road through the canyon. But that was too late for our comfort.

Unhappily the Club Ranch acquisition did not bring Ed the cow-and-calf capacity his new ambitions had envisioned. (Bonanza-land mentality.) To remedy that deficiency he went each year to Indian Creek in Utah, bought upward of a thousand head of yearlings from J. A. Scorup of the fabled Scorup-Somerville Cattle Company, and trailed them a couple of hundred miles to Beaver Park, a massive exercise in latter-day transhumance.

All this led him, at a time when cattle prices were beginning their pre-Depression skid, into more debt than he could handle. You simply had to think the gods were sore about something. Ed's associate died unexpectedly, and Ed felt compelled to borrow enough money to buy out his widow. A couple of years later, 1934 to be specific, Dwight died of polio while winding up a graduate degree in mining engineering at Stanford. Stomach cancer took Ed less than a year later. Mother had a classic nervous breakdown. That left me to run things. The bank suspected, correctly, that I hadn't learned enough ranching by age twenty-five (too much Eastern college) to handle so complex an operation amid the buffetings of the Great Depression. But after huddling together and wondering presumably, how *they'd* manage all that raw country, the vice presidents decided to let me try.

It was a good time, in retrospect. I learned to winter on the ranch, which I had not been able to do while away at college. I was married by then and had a son who didn't much care, at the time, whether the house we lived in at the Club Ranch had plumbing or not. (Today he has a summer cabin on a mesa below Telluride, where Ed Lavender had pastured his mules during his days of packing freight to the mines; for myself I never had the sense or the desire to make such a purchase.) I was able to ride, during that trial period, over the fantastic lands of the Scorup-Somerville Cattle Company, sleep in the caves the cowboys used, and gape at erosion-riven sandstone formations of such extraordinary quality that today a large part of them are embraced within Canyonlands National Park.

I couldn't hang on, which did not surprise even me. The bank took over and off I went with a saddle, a beat-up car, a wife and child. And a good education. And a point of view, although I can't say now whether I'd have held to the same outlook if the ranch had succeeded. Anyway, it was a good heritage. I had seen a whole way of life change, and I wanted to get it down on paper, which I sought to do in a book called *One Man's West.* After that came perspective—trying to put the specifics into broader pictures of the West. Trying to understand what had happened not just to me but to all the mountain country, the plateaus, the deserts.

Bonanza land. Translate the words as Old West. We skinned it as fast as we could, and it was wonderful, a challenge to our endurance and ingenuity, a joy in our accomplishments. Listen to the pop of champagne corks in Telluride. Listen to the shuffle of cards in the Denver Club. And now look. The trash dumps beneath the black mouths of the old tunnels. The road scars. The polluted streams. The clear-cut forests. The overgrazed ranges. The lost and threatened species. And the lovely canyons drowned under reservoirs so turbines can spin and ditches wind and the destruction go on at a still-faster pace.

We'll never be able to recapture the wildness. But surely we can avoid trashing any further the vast West whose magnificent sweep once exhilarated and inspired those who preceded us even while they (and we) were being twisted off track by the abundant opportunities that surrounded us. I still return to Telluride nearly every year to look at the peaks and waterfalls, to smell the meadows between the aspen groves, to listen to summer thunder crash between the canyon walls. In spite of a little uneasiness about the current, bonanza-style ski developments, I again feel the lift and love and vitality of that wondrous land. I know we can keep its harmonies *if we just will.* That can be our requiem for what we've had, as majestic in its resonances as the once-unspoiled world it celebrates.

WRIGHT MORRIS

Despite appearances, Wright Morris, at seventy-eight, has hardly settled down. Oh, he may seem comfortably nestled amid the collected clutter of his home in Mill Valley, California, that he shares with his wife, Jo, in the hills across the bay from San Francisco. But like his award-winning photographs, suggesting life and motion through objects, he conveys a sense of motion as well, never resting in one place or on one idea any longer than necessary, and once satisfied with what it has to give, he moves on.

We sat on the patio of his home of twenty-five years, less than a half hour commute from his former post of professor at California State University. He is an animated man, smaller than I imagined, who speaks with a big voice well honed by university lecture halls. And he spoke of change and motion, not only in the onset of urban sprawl encroaching upon his mountain home but throughout his entire life, starting with the early days with his widowed father out on the barren Nebraska plains, moving to the hectic competition of Chicago middle schools, on to Europe and California and finally to Pomona College in Claremont, in 1988, which he had attended himself as a young man, to teach his own books for a semester.

As we spoke it became apparent that Morris is, if nothing else, a man of paradox. There is an element of contradiction to him that made our discussion that day all the more fascinating. Take for example his literary career: despite

Wright Morris in the garden of his home in Mill Valley,
California, just north of San Francisco. (Photo by Joe Backes)

the impressive amount of praise and admiration from critics in the field, despite the long list of honors and awards (including the National Book Award in 1957 for his novel *The Field of Vision*), he has never been a commercially successful author. Critics are eager to point out Morris's technical mastery of language and his innovations in narrative technique, and Edward Abbey, writing in the *New York Times Book Review,* was prompted to refer to Morris as a "writer's writer." But the mass reading public, on the whole, is unaware of his work.

He laughed when I asked if there was ever any difficulty getting his books published because of this. "Yes, well, I have this problem because they expect me to sell," he grinned, "and then they find that I don't. There's always somebody to pick me up. . . . They think, each of these publishers, 'Now we'll sell him.' " Looking through a collection of his work reveals that for his early books Morris had almost as many publishers as he had titles, a veritable Who's Who of major American publishing houses, although he has been with the same house now for more than twenty years.

Yet in talking with Morris it becomes obvious that the commercial aspect of it all is not the point. For you see there is this paradox, too, about Morris: His writing, like his whole life, is an attempt to understand where he is going by getting a strong grasp on where he has been. As Jonathan Yardley described Morris in the *Washington Post Book World,* he is "one of those rare people who quite simply was born to write. He had no choice."

From Morris's point of view it does seem as if that is what he was meant to be doing all along. He shares the same simple plains upbringing of many of his contemporaries, like Wally Stegner and Frederick Manfred. And early on he fell into the pattern of change and motion that would eventually so heavily influence his work.

Born in 1910 in Central City, Nebraska, a small prairie town lying at the junction of two railroads, Morris was left, as he described it, "half an orphan" upon his mother's death five days after his birth. Eventually his father, then a station agent for the Union Pacific Railroad, led the young Morris from town to town throughout the Platte Valley as he sought a new wife and a new career. He found the former in Omaha, a woman "almost as young as the boy himself" (Morris admits in his autobiography), but with the exception of a brief attempt at being an entrepreneur (selling eggs to the railroad dining cars, which ended abruptly when the chickens died of cholera), he failed at the latter.

Morris's father then decided to head east, still pursuing the dream of becoming successful in business, and the family soon found itself in Chicago. It was there, in the wake of his father's continuing failures, that Morris first cultivated his independence. He spent some time working as a stock boy at Montgomery Ward and reigning as the undisputed Ping-Pong champ at the local YMCA. That period of his life, as Morris admits matter-of-factly, "displaces more water than its content." Those experiences held more weight at the time, he explained, because of the perspective of youth, though he valued the influence they would later have on his work.

It was here in our conversation that Morris showed a reluctance to talk about his past directly, giving me fair warning. "I'd better not get into this," he said, "because at this point my life gets very complicated. . . ." It seemed as though he had already considered certain parts of his life, written about them, and set them aside: a stay at a Seventh-Day Adventist college in northern California, touring the West by automobile with his father (the life of the picaro, which Morris would later incorporate into his first book, *My Uncle Dudley*), the early wanderer's voyage of discovery to Europe, college at Pomona and the marriage to his first wife, the beginning of his professional writing career, and the first photo books. The memories go on and on. They are all there in his three-volume memoir published between 1981 and 1984.

And although he didn't talk about it much, his past has had a strong influence on his work. He was already drawing on the adventures of his

Wright Morris.
(Photo by Joe Backes)

boyhood in *My Uncle Dudley,* writing himself into the story as "the Kid," touring across the West with his irreverent, unscrupulous uncle in a battered old car. The initial critical praise was good, and it continued, building momentum through seven more works, including *The Man Who Was There* in 1945, and the acclaimed *The Huge Season* in 1954. It was during this period—from the mid-thirties through the forties—that he became very actively engaged in his second love: taking photographs.

"The photography," he explains, "grew out of the writing, not the other way around." The parallels fascinate him, and he uses the static images of place in his pictures to mirror the characters revealed in his fiction. "They reflect the same. . . . You see I'm the same person in the photography as I am in the writing. The medium determines the difference." He has set aside his own photography now and is presently working on a volume of critical comments on the art.

In 1957 Morris received his first major award—a National Book Award for *The Field of Vision,* considered by many to be one of his most innovative and technically brilliant works—establishing his place on the literary horizon. It marked the first of a long series of coveted and prestigious honors, including the American Book Award for *Plains Song: For Female Voices* in 1981, and followed that same year by the *Los Angeles Times* Robert Kirsch Award for the whole body of his work—more than thirty works of fiction, photography, and critical essays, spread over almost fifty years.

Born to write? Yes, it would certainly seem so.

But perhaps born to teach as well. That is part of Morris's past also, and a part he is visibly proud of. He was fifty years old when he began to lecture, and in 1962 he joined the staff at California State University in San Francisco as a professor. He held that post for almost fifteen years.

"I think it is all of a piece . . . a very comprehensible piece," says Morris. "This is what I've been able to perceive in the last five years, when I have begun to wonder about what I've been doing all my life. And this is what I recently have been teaching, or attempting to share, with these young people at Pomona. I would have valued this tremendously when I was there."

And now it seems as if the traveling is done, at least in body. He seldom leaves home anymore, driving a short distance when he has to, forgoing lecturing engagements (and the inevitable flying it entails) altogether. But he hasn't stopped moving forward in spirit. His awareness is always focused ahead, to where he and his craft are going.

"Books," he admits with some concern, "are being phased out, into a kind of elitist activity." He is disturbed by the neon-and-chrome spectacle of modern culture. "I was one of those who believed that one day [words] would solve our problems—a feeling words could do anything, would do anything. I was wrong." It is the increasingly pop-oriented society that Morris abhors.

Despite all of the visual elements of Morris's work, despite the fact that he once referred to himself as a camera of sorts ("though who it is who clicks the shutter, I don't know"), it is language that he thrives on.

"I don't know what people will do if they suddenly stop using words," he says, "but using words is not really settling any of their problems." Another paradox, and one that Morris is still trying to come to grips with.

He sits there for a brief moment, a sparkle in his eyes, and you can almost hear his mind processing this information. This one may take him some time, but he is loving every minute of it.

And you can bet that when he comes up with an answer, Wright Morris will be happy to let us know.

C.B., 1988

*A homesteader's three children pose somewhat
uncertainly atop a horse. (Courtesy Special
Collections, University of Nevada-Reno Library)*

How I Put In the Time

My early years in the Platte Valley of Nebraska, so wide and flat I confused it with the Great Plains around it, had much in common with the boyhood of Isaac Babel in the Moldevanka ghetto of Odessa.

> As a boy [he wrote] I was given to lying. It was all due to my reading. My imagination was always on fire. I read in class, during recess, under the table, hidden by the folds of cloth that hung down to the floor.

I probably was given to fibbing with my father, at a loss as to how to get his attention. But what reading I did in Br'er Fox and Br'er Rabbit did not set my imagination on fire, if it so happened that I had one. I did forget to return most things I borrowed, including books. But I did share Babel's passion to be *under* something, and stay there until somebody found me. My father never found me. If I said to him, "You give up?" he was quick to give up. I hid under beds, clothes on the floor of closets, the porches of houses, the culverts of crossings, the lids of piano boxes, and piles of wet chicken feathers when I could find them. I hid for all of one day in an empty cookie barrel in Eoff's basement. Nobody found me. I'd probably still be there, but I got scared first, then hungry.

Nor did my father, who ran the railroad station, a purple stain on his lips from the indelible pencils, ever bounce me on his knee, tell me a bedtime story, or tickle me until I got the hiccups. When he kissed me I got the taste of Sen-Sen, or the bitter flavor of the indelible pencils. I was open to almost anything, I think, but to my knowledge not much ever happened. The one time I snitched forty cents from his pocket, all of it in thin dimes, he didn't miss them.

Some of this was good training for a future writer of fiction, but it was not much fun. The skills of fibbing (which I was pretty good at), along with peering, prying, and spying on people dressing, were those that I felt free to develop. Knotholes, keyholes, squinting down the barrels of air guns, or being suddenly snatched—as I approached danger—helped me to get quick, memorable glances of what I had just turned my back on, or anything that might surprise or engulf me. Some of these things are the ones I remember. In this category are the close escapes I had on Halloweens. During the war my father might have gone to if he had not had me to look after, these big hooting rascals would come in from the country to load two-seater privies onto flat wagons, and move them from one town to another. They put the big ones in a circle at the center of the square, NO MAN'S LAND painted on the doors. This enigmatic message was the first I couldn't get off my mind.

Also on my mind, like a bull's-eye, was the hole somebody had poked at the exact center of the map on the wall of the railroad station. The hole was right where I was standing when I stood in the lobby looking at the map. During the years I was looking at it the hole was at the center of the United States, at the navel of the world. Around this bull's-eye, like a target, with other holes poked in it, I could see the town of Kearney to the west, Aurora to the south, St. Paul and Palmer up to the north, and as much of Omaha as I wanted between 29th and Farnam and the bridge over the river to Council Bluffs. That was pretty much the heart of the matter. The misunderstanding that developed later was when I ran into people, some of them girls, from places as far away

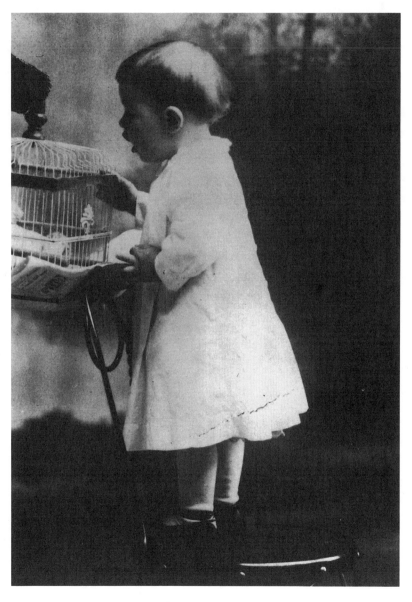

Wright Morris in 1912, when he was about two and a half years old. (From the Morris family collection)

as Ohio and Indiana, who felt pretty much as I did about places with names like Winesburg and Oolitic. For most people I knew the navel of the world seemed to be wherever it was they came from, even after I had explained it to them. To really pinpoint it, it's a bit to the south of the forty-first parallel, to the west of the ninety-eighth meridian, and as many as ten to fifteen miles from where it sometimes rained, but most of the times it didn't. A simpler way to spot it was about an hour's walk from what was once the Lone Tree stop of the Pony Express. They've got a concrete stump of the tree there now to mark the spot.

A lot of this would have been different, as you can well imagine, if I had not been an *only* child, and to make it even worse, half an orphan. The half that might have kept an eye on me—the loving, caring, white-haired woman who listened to my prayers, washed, mended and ironed my drop-seat rompers—mostly had her eyes on the choir she sang and hummed along with on Sunday. My own mother had died five days after I was born. One of her older sisters, Violet, offered to adopt and raise me, but her father moved his own remaining family of daughters to a Seventh-Day Adventist settlement near Boise, Idaho. I would first set eyes on all of them, by winter lamplight, twenty years to the day after my mother's death.

Unknown to me at the time, the view down the tracks into the wild blue yonder was not due west, as I thought, but southerly, into the face of the prevailing wind. This long dog-leg bend in the valley accommodated a river almost a mile wide in some stretches, but only in the spring, running with water. In overdue time I would learn that a quantity of mountain water was flowing eastward, but *under* the river rather than in it, water that I had heard described as "artesian." The wide riverbed itself, seen from infrequent bridges, was a sandy wash of shallow rivulets and bleached-out sandbars, mirrorlike pools of minnows and others too small to fish, plus suckholes and sandpits known to gobble up boys in drop-seat rompers. In even longer, overdue time,

I would learn that the word Nebraska, of Indian origin, was best translated as Shallow Water. That would not be the first nor the last bit of lore I would come on in books, once I had become a writer of fiction, sometimes reduced to the craft of reading. There were no books in the house I "grew up in"—*Br'er Rabbit* I brought home from the library. The first book that attracted my eye was in the farmhouse of my Uncle Harry, near Norfolk. It was bound in red cloth, and the author's name, Harold Bell Wright, was stamped on the cover. Until that moment the name *Wright,* on lease from my grandfather, had been one of the impediments of my boyhood—what *else* can you call a boy named Wright? That this name was on a book, and that the title of the book, *When a Man's a Man,* had been chosen to flatter, intrigue, and provoke me, while forever eluding my comprehension—it might fairly be said that this unread novel *did* influence the future writer.

Long past the middle of life, in that void between the looted past and the receding future, it would be brought to my attention that the *West,* real and imaginary, visible on the map and in the wild blue yonder, was largely a landscape of my own invention. Like my beloved Uncle Dwight, my mother's adoring brother, who single-handedly invented the dust bowl on a farm in the Texas panhandle, I had come too late for the West of my longing, but too early for the West that was emerging, currently on hold on the back burner. *This* West began at the beginning—that imaginary line where the long grass country became the short grass, with more growth below the surface than above it. Confounding such beginnings, I was born in a town that the settlers had called Lone Tree—there being *one* tree, a cottonwood, on the near side of the river, briefly the site of a Pony Express stop—but this remarkably apt and evocative image, so appealing to a much later generation, was not at all what the wives of settlers from Ohio, Illinois, Indiana, and everywhere else had in mind on their arrival. Soon enough it was changed to Central City, a reading of the compass that came easily to men who had been inspired by Horace

Card players pass the time at a saloon in California.
(Courtesy California State Library, Sacramento)

Greeley. They had "gone West." The West began wherever they had gone.

Had it been an oversight, on the part of those who bred and raised me, to avoid all views of the mountains, Indian reservations, or those hideouts all over the place known to have been frequented by horse thieves and cattle rustlers? It so happened that the barber who cut my father's hair, and trimmed my mother's, had come up from Texas on the Chisholm Trail, but tiring of the saddle and the early morning rising he had stopped off in Chapman and become a barber. Not a word of this, of course, did I get from my father, both his eyes and his ears on the girls he could see—cranked up in the barber chair—backing down from the buggies at the hitch bar. I got it all, and then some, from Eddie Cahow, the barber, who had recognized me as my father's son from the wave in my hair. My mother's eyes did not escape him either, he being one of the many young men who had admired her. Only my father, he openly suggested, spared me from having the name of Cahow. From the seat of the chair where she had once sat, he could look to the low rise to the southeast, with the windbreak of trees, where she lay buried. Had I known—what tempted him to ask me?—that I had had a brother by the name of Fayette? I had not. A much smaller stone marked his grave, and he had died before he had need of a haircut.

I took many photographs of Cahow's barbershop, with the ornate grillwork and solid oak woodwork that set off the First National Bank of Chapman, in the back of the shop, from the benches, chairs, wall-to-wall calendars, the sink for shampoos, the counter for the bottles of red and green sweet-smelling tonics, the cases for the razors with the razor that had shaved William Jennings Bryan on its own towel, on its own shelf. Not to mention both the peanut and the gum machines, the postcards edging the mirror from far-traveling clients, and the photograph of the Chapman baseball team in uniforms provided by a laundry supplier in Grand Island. Cahow had been the mascot of that team, and sat cross-legged at the front, the ball and bat in his lap.

An obviously prosperous Western family uses its automobile as a power source to auger grain into a silo. (Courtesy local history collection, Pike's Peak Library District)

So it was in Chapman, ten miles down the tracks, where the sunrise flared on the rippled wall of the grain elevator, that *my* West actually began. On a Memorial Day my father hitched up the buggy and drove his "family"—the child and the elderly lady, who held the child in her lap, the hamper of lunch between them, the buggy shadow concealing the horse going west, then, homeward bound, casting a leaky shade. In the cemetery I picked up sandburs, which had to be painfully plucked from the stockings. Led back to the pump, to the shade of the buggy, we ate fried chicken from the picnic hamper, and drank too much of the cool water my father pumped into the tin cup wired to the nozzle. I had no "likeness" of this child, no *picture,* until one of my cousins found in a shoe box a group photograph taken in 1915. The mixed bag of sons and daughters of the middle border was more than likely somebody's birthday party. Among the midgets seated at the front I recognize myself. A plump-faced puppy, hair parted at the middle, the jug-eared head too large for the body— my lips are parted to assist in what I know to be my adenoidal breathing. Their memorable removal—another stirring story—would be delayed until my guardian angel was no longer there to obstruct the operation. That adventure would take me clear to Grand Island, followed by a drunken spree of drinking Welch grape juice, my favorite. What I had lacked all of my adult life was the *scale* provided by this photograph. Little wonder that I had not explored the river, such as it was, or when the locomotive stood panting in the station I had failed to take my stand on the cow catcher. I lived to see this train, with me on it, outrun by a team of ordinary horses, the driver pulling them up at the crossing to thumb his nose at me and the conductor. On the high embankment the train was going so slowly I could see its shadow, like a paper cutout, crossing the field of corn stubble with the sunlight on the windows, big inky clouds of smoke puffing from the funnel stack.

How to share my allegiance with *two* real railroads would prove to be an insoluble problem. One was there daily, to set the clocks by, the other one came and went when it felt like it—the only way I had of knowing was the bell clanging, the dogs barking until Mrs. Riddlemosher told them to shut up.

The first piece of paved road, all of it concrete, better for bicycle riders than skaters, began on the east side of the station and went straight east halfway to Schuyler. At the time I was too young to grasp the radical nature of this improvement. A town headed west, at its inception, and looked to the west the way people look to the future, wheeled around like an engine on a turntable to face in the opposite direction. This was not lost on my father, but Mr. Riddlemosher felt there was something personal about it. He had been working with me on a fighter airplane made of matchsticks, with rubber bands to work the propeller, but he more or less lost interest with the first rumors of an armistice. I didn't lose my interest in building a fighter plane, but I soon got tired of winding up the propeller. In a field cleared of stubble near the river, where a plane could do the loop-the-loop and not fall on anybody, Gerald Cole and I watched one come in to land rocking like a kite. We could see the whir of the propeller, and the way it jumped around like a chicken with its head off. The aviator wore a helmet with goggles, but I was not seized with the desire to be like him. When he offered to take a boy for a spin, I did not volunteer. I wasn't what you would call a coward, exactly, but neither was I the first one to take a dare. The one dare I took, to dive from the bridge into the river, I took so long to do I got cold and shivery with goose bumps. Ten years later, on a dare I had made to myself in Sterling, Colorado, I ran out from the bushes and shrubs along the tracks to catch a free ride east on a freight train. Hard as it was for me to do, I did it. It was a promise I had made, and I had to keep it. It was all I could do to get a grip on the ladder, and pull myself up to the top of the freight car, where one of the ice hatches was open and light from the sky lit up the darkness. Two of the faces below me were so black I saw only the eyes. They weren't really black faces, as I thought, but white faces blackened by the smoke and cinders. One of them beckoned to me to come and join them, which was what I did. I was on my way to Europe, and had to learn to take things one at a time.

What my boyhood had been *like*—how I looked to those who looked at me—I had little idea. I had not been scooped to a lap to look at an album of pictures. No piano, dresser, or side table held objects framed for contemplation. No mirror captured for me my image. I do see clearly the scales in the station lobby, but not the child who stands there, clutching a penny, or the weight on the dial the wagging needle will point to. Circumstantial evidence, not beyond refutation, speaks of a boy with doughnut curls hanging about his ears until they were lopped off with sheep shears. From a more verifiable perspective, beneath the porch of the house I lived in, I peered through the side slats to watch the summer showers puff the dust as they came marching down the street. Or did I *write* that, then come to believe it? Examples of this

A homesteader and her son in their simple frontier shack. (Courtesy Utah State Historical Society)

sort are too numerous to mention. What I *do* know is that whatever I saw through the slats had the fragrant moistness of a breeze blowing through sprinklers.

In a town of almost twenty-five hundred people, already so big it was served by two railroads, it still made do with one rusty track siding for the yearly Chautauqua and Hagenbeck and Wallace circus. In the cages on the flat cars the big cats roared. The elephants were watered, maybe two or three of them, by barefooted, snot-nosed boys who would later crawl under the tent flaps to watch the circus for free between the legs of the customers squatted in the bleachers. Back from the clearing for the tent, back from the horses and buggies, in the tall grass at the foot of the railroad embankment, those big boys and girls I somehow never set an eye on trampled the grass flat and left hairpins for me to look for later. Seated on a spring seat they had taken from a buggy I had time to think about it, but I came to no conclusions.

Once I found a silver dollar, which was so much money there wasn't anyplace for me to spend it. What did I do with it? I've thought and thought about it, but I can't remember.

I *just* now remember, for the first time, my father seated on the buckboard of a small wagon, with me sitting on a bundle of hay behind him. The moment before he had given me a silver dollar to go into a store and buy myself a dollar watch. Did I buy the watch? I don't remember. What I remember is the heft of the silver dollar. What had moved my father to give me so much money, and then wait for me to go and spend it? What I remember ends there. That's it. When I really needed money for a nut Hershey, or a long whip of licorice, I would swipe it from the pocket of the pants he left to hang on the bedpost. I never took so much I thought he would miss it. Pennies mostly, maybe a dime in a pinch. Being an only child, plus half an orphan, may encourage such behavior, since I didn't have an older sister to catch me at it.

When I really put my mind to it, I don't seem to know how I put in the time. I had hours and hours of it every day, and days and weeks of it every summer, but I don't have any memory of it weighing on my hands, as I did later. If I had eight or ten cents, I would go spend it on banana candy, or the whips of licorice I liked to chew on and spit from the tops of freight cars. One thing I never tired of doing was trying to figure out why the streets in our town seemed to run every which way, but were orderly, with square corners, in towns like Schuyler and Columbus. If the streets and the tracks don't cross at right angles, how do you ever figure out where you're really at?

I did finally figure it out, however, about forty years later. It didn't just come to me. I was writing a story about a small-town boy who had a snuffling problem, because of his adenoids. In another place, or another time, some-body would have *done* something about it—but in that time, and in *that* place, it seemed okay for a small boy to snorfel. When it didn't get better he was finally driven almost twenty-five miles, to a town like Grand Island, where the ether they gave him made him so thirsty he thought he would die till they gave him some bottles of grape juice. Knowing he would drink too much, and probably whoop it up, they put him in the back of the buggy, where he did just that, but it hardly mattered.

That was the story, and thinking about it led me to solve the messed-up street problem. The town I was living in, as I may have said, had not just one but two railroads. The C, B & Q, which had just one set of tracks, with grass that grew between them in the rainy season, came out of the bluffs south of the Platte and crossed the Union Pacific at an angle that soon led to complica-tions. Streets parallel to the C, B & Q, which they had to be, were not parallel to very much else. Working back from that fact I was able to puzzle out why the main street of the town, which came in from the east, made a dogleg right in the square in order to leave the town parallel with the Union Pacific. A smarter, more observant boy than I seemed to have been should have figured that out, but I didn't. I could have *seen* that on the railroad map in the station,

The Fourth of July parade heads up Main Street in Virginia City,
circa 1909. (Courtesy Special Collections, University of Nevada-Reno Library)

if I had just known for what I was looking. In point of fact, both according to the compass, and to the map on the wall of the station, the C, B & Q, coming up from Aurora, was headed due north until it crossed the U.P., and made this dogleg toward the sandhills. I lived with that perplexity most of my life. It will probably explain a good deal about me that I have not got around to explaining to my readers but has been, as they well know, an inexhaustible source of my fiction. Misapprehensions of this sort, dilemmas of this magnitude, are the stuff of life to a writer of fiction, and the stuff of fictions that proves to be his life. Like my father, I never really put behind me the two railroads that intersected my boyhood.

Another thing—for all the talk about the treeless plains, the sea of grass, etc., to which I have added both words and pictures, my boyhood was an oasis of elm-shaded street. and grass-clogged culverts. As I was four-and-one-half feet tall in my bare feet, a foot shorter than the corn that tasseled around me, the glimpses I caught of the horizon down the railroad tracks had some, but not much, attraction for me. From my point of observation, under the porch, I checked and double-checked the arrival of the Jewel's Tea Wagon with the vanilla essence I could sniff the cork of. Left to my own devices, and I had few others, I found them remarkably time-consuming. The time in which I would soon grow to take an interest I could stretch like the squeaky rubber of a balloon to where I could see my knuckles through it. Time pieces that eluded me, for the time being—their wear and tear, their blight, their dry rot, all of it that I would treasure as time's ruin—I neither cared nor knew much about. What it came down to, wherever I found it, was what I felt a reluctance to turn away from, that I would one day turn into a salvage operation. I was seeing this time wherever I looked, before I knew what I was seeing. Right there before me, peeling from a barn, from which the paint had already peeled, were the tattered strips, like torn banners, of last year's Hagenbeck and Wallace circus, with the girl on the flying trapeze more enticing than the circus itself.

Why did this town of twenty-five hundred people, with everything to gain and so little to lose, not grow and expand in every direction, like Kearney did and Grand Island hoped to? One reason was that *traveling* men, from Omaha and Kansas City (I had not yet heard of Chicago), with their gladstone bags and creaky cowhide luggage, had to get off the train so far down the tracks they were closer to the Burlington and Quincy than they were to the Union Pacific station. They joked about that with my father, who sometimes walked down the tracks to help them. When they did finally get to the station, the only place for them to stay looked like an abandoned warehouse. Over the back door, where they went in and out, an electric bulb lit up the word HOTEL. They had to walk through the kitchen, carrying their bags, to get to the desk and lobby at the front. When they got to it, Mr. Riddlemosher might be sitting in one of the rockers, working on an airplane made of matches. There may have been *something* across the street, but the fact is I don't remember. The front door to the lobby, set in catty-corner, was eight cement steps up from the street, each step so high ladies refused to take them. If I remember correctly—and I was often in it, to sell tinfoil to Mr. Riddlemosher—there was no place to sit, no place to spit, and no cigar counter with a hooded flame to light a cigar. There was a counter, too high for me to see over, with pigeonholes at the back for mail and room keys. The salesmen who came back, which were not many, kept the keys in their pockets to save all the trouble. I have dwelt on this lobby in a novel, somewhere, and hope the interested reader will recognize it. To get the bloom of a novel it helps to read all the good parts twice.

At a time every Western man smoked and gambled—spitting indoors was something of an option. My father neither smoked, drank, gambled nor swore, but he liked to sit and talk in a good lobby. A good one had palm trees in tubs at the front, with a tile floor all the way back to the desk. Without a lobby from where to watch what was going on, without a lobby where something of interest might happen, a town could have half a dozen or more good railroads but in no time at all none of the trains would stop. Even before I knew anything else, I knew that.

My father didn't smoke, but he liked to sit where he could watch the girl at the cigar counter slide back the lid of the glass case so the smoker could help himself to a cigar. The smoker would let the girl snip off the end he would chew on, then light it up with big puffs at the hooded lighter. I'm not making this up. I once sat with my father in a lobby with fans in the ceiling, and saw it all the way he did, how the big smokers would tip her, if she was pretty, blowing out clouds of smoke it was hard to see through. That part of it my father didn't much like, and stepped up to the counter to say so. The cigar-counter girl couldn't believe it when he said he didn't smoke. "Have one on me," she said, shaking the cup of dice, but she could see it wasn't the cigar he wanted. What he wanted was a new mother for me, a wife for himself.

From Omaha, in an Overland car he had left the train to buy in Columbus, my father brought me Gertrude, the young woman he had met at the cigar counter. She held out her arms toward me, and gave me a big red-lipped smile. She was nearer my own age than my father's, and we got along fine.

That summer we lived in Schuyler, then in Kearney, then in a farmhouse near the embankment where the C, B & Q went north to St. Paul. The elderly woman who had taken care of me took care of all else. My father raised leghorn chicks in incubators to lay day-old eggs for the dining-car service, but nobody had told him about the cholera. From our upstairs window Gertrude and I could see the leghorn pullets, like piles of white feathers, huddled in the corners of the chicken runs. A pit as wide and deep as a basement had to be dug behind the sheds to bury the dead ones. Those that didn't die my father sent to his brother Harry, on his farm near Norfolk, who refused to take them from the railroad platform to mix in with his own Plymouth Rocks. We couldn't go out in the yard because of the smell of the quicklime until the chickens were buried and the sheds were fumigated. My father bought us a Victrola, and an album of records, to help us pass the time. The record Gertrude liked the most, and liked to sing along with, was about a yellow tulip, which she said I was, and a red, red rose, which I knew she was. One day my father, his hair smelling of quicklime when he stooped to kiss me, came to the door to ask us how we would like to live in Omaha. "How would you two like to live in Omaha?" he said, and we both said we would like it fine.

I would begin a new life in Omaha, a big town with streetcars and stores with escalators, but first we were in this hotel room, somewhere, to get away from the influenza epidemic. My father had turned from the mirror to reach for his collar, looped around the bedpost with his tie still in it. Later on, to save time, he would leave the knot loose in his tie. With his back to me, so I could help with the collar button, he said, "Kid, our lives would be different if your mother had lived, and don't you forget it."

What I remember of that is my father speaking to me, for the first time, as an equal, but until most of my life had been lived I didn't recall him saying that *our* lives would be different. I was not only young at the time, but ignorant.

I had never actually set eyes on my mother, but I had heard how her brother, my uncle Dwight, would take her on these buggy rides along the river, his Winchester rifle on the seat between them. If he wanted to shoot it, he had to stop the horse, but she could shoot while the buggy was moving. If there were no chicken hawks or rabbits for her to shoot at, she would aim at the glass insulators on the telephone poles. If she hit one, the shards of the bottle-green glass would splatter all around, like water. I wasn't there, but I can see all of that just as if I were.

On my father's railroad pass—which I just now remember—he and my mother went to San Francisco on their honeymoon, from where he wired Eddie Cahow, the barber, to deposit fifty dollars to his account at the bank. It was Eddie Cahow, not my father, who told me that, the bank being right there at the back of his shop.

CLYDE RICE

In 1984, at the age of eighty-one, Clyde Rice had his first-ever book published, an event undertaken with little fanfare and even less financial promise by tiny, literary-minded Breitenbush Books of Portland, Oregon. The spirited narrative of Rice's life from the time he was sixteen until he was thirty-two, at the bottom of the Great Depression, it was titled, for some reason nobody seems quite clear about today, *A Heaven in the Eye*.

There is nothing altogether unique about such a thing; it has taken other aspiring writers burdened with more than the normal ration of hard luck many years, sometimes even the major part of their lifetimes, to find their way into print. What is unusual here, however, is that Rice was anything but a frustrated writer despairing of his big opportunity. He hadn't written anything, in fact, before that first book, hadn't even thought of writing seriously until he was already well into his seventies. Oh, he had been turning out a line or two of poetry on occasion throughout most of his life, "just to get it out, get it done with." He had even, several times, published some of it on men's room walls. "One poem, I remember, survived three washings over a couple of years and almost made it through a new coat of paint." But that was hardly real writing, the kind real writers do.

A former star of youthful promise in the U.S. Forest Service, former ferry-boat deckhand and commercial fisherman, former goat rancher, stump farmer,

Clyde Rice. (Photo by Joe Backes)

boat builder and businessman, former just about everything you could possibly imagine, Rice had simply been too busy doing other things—and failing miserably, if the truth be told, at every one of them—even to think about his chances of becoming a creator of books.

He and his wife of forty-two years, Ginny, relived those years one rainy afternoon in the comfortable living room of their home, a rammed-earth structure on the outskirts of Portland that Clyde built with his own hands more than fifty years ago. All around were signs that the Rices, both of them, have long had a hands-on love of the visual arts; several of Ginny's watercolors decorate the walls. There is a life-size wooden bust of her done by Clyde, as well as a scale model of the sailing sloop he once built in the backyard. Atop an attached building, over the garage, is a spacious studio originally designed for her but which he has since claimed and does all his writing in, working at an ancient black Smith-Corona that looks as if it should come with a green eyeshade and sleeve garters.

The early years. My, yes. How the memories go on.

The Forest Service job began when he was just sixteen, said Rice, and quickly led to a promise by the U.S. Secretary of Agriculture himself of a college scholarship if he would make the service his career; the man had been greatly impressed by Clyde's prowess in identifying and diagraming seedlings in a forest burn—the devil's own job, even for an experienced hand. This, the promise, ended for all practical purposes the day Clyde stumbled upon his ranger boss exploring a bit of wild and scenic nature, so to speak, with the young wife of an elderly California senator. Within weeks a scathingly negative character report, signed by the ranger, permanently derailed not only the scholarship but Rice's job, too.

The pattern, thus established, seemed to repeat itself over and over across the years: early promise, followed by some twist of fate or collision with the hard underside of human nature, followed in turn by disaster once more. It never seemed to end.

There was the time, in San Francisco, when he had the brilliant idea of supplying goat's milk to the city's hospitals and customers allergic to cow's milk; nobody else was doing it. He even found a dairy willing to distribute the product for him. So over the next year he bought goats, leased land, built barns and processing sheds, spent every spare cent he could beg or borrow on the project—and just days before beginning operation saw the city enact a new certification law that in effect legislated goat's milk out of existence. He spent the next year eating the goats and looking for other work.

Or the time in rural Oregon that he bought eighty acres of stumps for four hundred dollars and started a stump ranch—clearing the land by cutting the old growth and selling it as cordwood, expecting in the end that he would have a prime piece of property ready for cultivation. Then he missed a payment by scant days and lost it all, still only half worked over. The former owner, it turned out, had learned that there was a fair gravel quarry on the property and had made a deal with the county to sell the land all over again the minute Rice faltered on his contract.

Or the time he invented "respighi," a new ice-cream flavor made of grapefruit oil ("one of the cheapest things on the market; they've got too much of it") and a little sweet cherry and pistachio, and took out a copyright on it and had it all but sold to the Carnation Company before one of their independent dairy contractors shot the deal down, trying to reserve the flavor at a cut rate for his own use. Or the time he built the fishing boat, spending a year and a half on it, and launched it at San Pedro high on hope and the tuna simply dried up, resulting in the worst fishing season in decades (the boat still plies the waters off Mexico, but under someone else's ownership). Or the time he built the sawmill on the mountain slope and almost immediately lost it to bad times and big-money competition.

But the worst years, Rice said, were probably those he worked for his father, some twenty of them off and on, at pauper's wages, with the understanding that the family business—the Acme Flavoring Company, manufacturer of food extracts—would someday be his. It never happened, of course. His father, in his old age, sold the business out from under him, and Clyde was forced to go to work for the new owners at $1.75 an hour to keep food on the table, doing all those things he had been learning to do so diligently through the years.

"I got so that I didn't believe in myself at all," said Rice. "My hand would tremble when I was holding the graduates and using the equipment they make extracts with. I became terribly insecure."

"I felt so sorry for him," said Ginny. "He had had so much bad luck for so very long."

Clyde Rice. (Photo by Joe Backes)

It is a terrible story, of course, a virtual Stations of the Cross of everybody's worst career nightmares, and you would expect Rice to be scarred by it today, embittered by the unremitting disappointment. But he doesn't seem to be. In fact there is in him an almost joyous, leprechaunlike quality totally at odds with his earlier lack of self-confidence: a spirit of impish fun that draws its nourishment from his animated visual imagination. He is constantly creating verbal cartoon sketches of events from his past life, people he has known, things he has seen. And when he scores just right on one of them, when the picture rings clear and the message is inarguably true, his face lights up with a blazing smile that suggests he hasn't a care in the world.

It was after the mill failed, in the middle-to-late 1970s, that he began finally to write.

He started after undergoing an operation on a bad knee that didn't quite take; he couldn't walk on it and was forced to sit around for a time in idleness. He found himself committing to paper the events of his life before he met Ginny, when he and his first wife, Nordi, were starting out, trying to survive the Depression. The manuscript grew.

"A doctor who lives up the road dropped by one day and said, 'What are you doing?' A curious guy," said Clyde. "So I showed him. He liked it. It made me feel good, and I kept on writing.

"Well, I thought after a while, maybe I'd better get some professional help on this. So I called up a lady I know who teaches at a community college, and she advised me to see this man she said was a very clever poet. I tried to call him, but his line was busy, and I thought, 'Oh, heck! I'll call Reed College while I'm waiting.' I did, and when someone answered I said, 'Have you got a poet or a novelist on the staff?' They said they did and I said, 'Will you put him on the phone.' I didn't care.

"And that's how I first met Gary Miranda."

It proved to be a turning point—belated though it might have been—in Rice's frustrating life.

"To make a long story short," Rice went on, "he agreed to take a look at what I had done, and when I brought it down to him—the start of *A Heaven in the Eye*—he liked it. 'This is professional writing,' he told me. Right away I knew I had to grab this guy. Everybody else had always said, 'Why don't you take up other work?' All down through the years they had always wanted me to take up other work, whatever I was doing. Here finally was someone who could see I was professional."

In the end, it turned out to be a little more complicated than that. Miranda—part-time professor of creative writing, published poet, ex-Jesuit—worked with Rice for almost three years before the manuscript was ready for publication. Breitenbush, who had published one of Miranda's books, agreed to bring it out.

Then one day Miranda came across a brochure announcing that the Western States Arts Foundation—composed of the tax-supported arts councils of fourteen Western states—was planning to establish a biennial series of literary awards it would present to outstanding books by Western writers published in the West, and on a hunch he submitted Rice's manuscript for consideration. *A Heaven in the Eye* was named the first winner in the category of creative nonfiction; Rice that spring was flown to Washington, D.C., for the Western States Book Awards ceremony and presented with his prize check.

Other good things began happening. Poet and novelist James Dickey praised the book as "an astonishing work"; the *Kirkus Reviews* called it "a generous, underdone slice of life," and the trade journal *Publishers Weekly* called attention to its "memorable insights." Avon, the paperback publisher, offered fifty thousand dollars for reprint rights. Two years later Rice's second book, titled *Night Freight,* was published by Breitenbush and outsold the first one. A sequel to *A Heaven in the Eye,* covering Rice's life from 1934 to the present, is scheduled to appear.

He continues to write, driven, he said, by something that has been there all his life: an inner urge goading him to produce, to look to his own creativity. "If you write a poem right or build a boat right or kiss a lady right you can satisfy that urge for a while."

He smiled that incredible smile. "And that's just about the nicest thing there is."

C.B., 1988

Leaving the Fold: A Boyhood in Oregon

I was born, they tell me, on a July morning in 1903, a fourth generation Oregonian, a native of the salubrious valley of the Willamette. The Willamette parallels the Pacific Ocean, which lies fifty miles to the west. Between, the coast-range mountains gentle the marine atmospheres from the furies of wind and weather.

Our home on the outskirts of Portland was in a district where the brush and second-growth fir of old logged-off land had not yet been worn completely away. I had a mother of monumental will and dainty ways and two sisters, one a tomboy, the other a throwback in appearance to a bit of Indian ancestry. A Welsh colonel in Washington's Continental Army didn't go back to Massachusetts after the British left, but found his way through Cumberland Gap, married a Cherokee woman and settled down in Tennessee—Colonel Rhys (Rice), squaw man.

My mother's grandfather, a Devonshire farmer, had brought his large family over to New York City, from whence his six stalwart sons had scattered to the West. One, my mother's father, had worked his way across to Oregon with pick and shovel, on the payroll of the railroad that would tie Portland into the nation.

As for my memories of early childhood, they are confused with snapshots my mother kept. These photographs of children at tea parties or standing

Clyde at age nine with Helen, eight, and
Valerie, six. (From the Rice family collection)

beside horses and of myself, spruced up and posed with my sisters, are tiny bits of family history. They filter in among other memories in which I was the camera.

My grandmother had a tale of me at age three and a half in that spitting time, the age of chewing tobacco, in which she was pleased to say I didn't ape the common people who spat on the sidewalk, but with an aloof and supercilious waddle moved to the curb with my synthetic expectoration. I heard about it so much I almost believe I saw it. I also have been and am affected by a photograph taken by a real photographer in his studio, with a background of mountains and bowers and little me in a Lord Fauntleroy suit (practically a pinafore) and a great, wide-brimmed sailor hat and soft leather baby shoes staring truculently at the birdie. I suppose I get this picture mixed into my grandmother's yarn and think of it as a memory of an incident, when really it's a concoction that helps me see the spitting incident. In any case I think of my childhood with real hills and mountains always in the background, their imagined hazards and adventures beckoning me toward my future life.

When I was five I was the proud owner of an Indian tepee, feathered headdress, and bow and arrow. One day I chanced to look up and see a large hawk circling overhead. I ran into the tepee and brought out my bow and arrow but, looking up at the hawk, felt very inadequate with such weaponry. I darted back and came out once more with my feathered headdress on and carrying a large spear with a heavy stone point that an old man had made for me. This I heaved up at the circling bird—oh, about seven feet into the air. It fell back, striking me a bruising blow on the shoulder. Though the hawk was at least two hundred feet up and my spear had gone up less than ten feet, I was satisfied, having engaged a bird of prey in battle.

And so it went.

My father, a traveling salesman of groceries, was away from home a lot during the week. In livery stables he found rigs and drivers to take him to the

Two ladies take a spin on an early plank road through redwood country in the Pacific Northwest. (Courtesy California State Library, Sacramento)

next town, and from odd little steamers he worked the coastal and river communities. Until he got his Model T Ford in 1913, transportation was an expensive and delaying process. With the Ford he certainly learned the ruts of the roads more intimately, often arriving at Hardscrabble or Peola messed from his tire changing but, under the coveralls he carried for such hazards, still presentable, as a traveling man should be. He was exceedingly honest and soon was trusted throughout the state by his customers. When he went into business for himself, the goodwill he had built up helped him with his new endeavor—manufacturing extracts and flavorings.

I remember, out for a ride, my father gripping the wheel as he got his Ford up to thirty-seven miles an hour. "Look, children!" said my mother proudly from the front seat. "See how the fence posts whip by!" But my father would stop at every railroad crossing, edge up to it and, looking carefully both ways, hurry across. And on turns on narrow roads he always blew his horn to let those coming the opposite way know that he was advancing in their direction. Many blind curves had a sign at each end that said, "Sound your Klaxon"—a very loud horn of those days. Sound your Klaxon! How it brings back the dust and the deep mud, the isinglass side curtains, and the crude headlights of the past.

Our world was sleep and play and school, and our mother reading to us each night. From 7:00 until 8:00 P.M. in our house Robinson Crusoe worked on his leather umbrella. Sir Walter Scott's novels moved at their regal pace. Our mother read *Huckleberry Finn, The Iliad* and *The Odyssey, El Cid* (we knew each knight who sat at King Arthur's round table as well as we did our first cousins), and for my sisters she read *Little Women.* In time I became a full-blown romantic, never again to see things as they are. Or at least never again to see things as nonromantic people see them—though if what they see is truly the way things are is a splendidly debatable subject.

My father had bought two building lots in Irvington and two in Laurelhurst, two fashionable suburbs. He wanted to build a house, but my mother didn't want us to be raised with (what a term!) "select" people. She believed passionately in democracy and a soon-to-be-perfected world. So we bought a house in a nonstatus district, "where our children," she said, "can mingle with all God's children." We did.

With four or five other boys I played in a small tract of timber east of us. We had battles with boys from another tract to the south. These battles were fought with the cones of the Douglas fir, which we soaked in ponds to make them hard. I made shields for myself and followers, using slats from boxes and pieces of hose for arm- and handholds, attaching sacks to them to hold a supply of ammunition. Soon our opponents had shields, too, and the mock battles we had after school and at noon were quite complicated affairs, with ambushes and flanking and other maneuvers.

Games around the schoolyard were tied to the seasons. Marbles—or migs, as we called them—would hold the attention of every boy for a month, then it would be tops or hoops or Pom-Pom Pull-Away—a marvelous game in which boys formed two lines sixty feet apart with a guard in the center. The aim was to run to the opposite side without being tagged by the guard. Once tagged, you joined him in the center space. When all were tagged the game started over. Artful dodging was the requisite. Then running races and wrestling or another game we just called Sticks, which consisted of slamming a pointed stick with much force into the ground and then having the next boy try to slam his own stick down in such a way that it would knock the first loose while his stayed planted in the mud. Of course baseball and soccer were played as well as handball, my forte, but the strange games that we played without formal school sanction still fascinate me.

The scene I see is of boys out on a muddy piece of ground in pairs carrying out a game of Sticks as if life depended on it. Mist encircles the field, rain is falling, and—knickers up and knickers down, clothing twisted every

Clyde at age eleven poses in his homemade cart with a pet chipmunk on his shoulder. (From the Rice family collection)

which way—the boys strive in a light verging on deep twilight. The southern half of the sky is black with a great storm cloud that, moving up over them, is about to give birth to a deluge, but the boys are unaware of any of this. Then, as suddenly as the game began, it would disband and the usual monkey business of the schoolyard would prevail once more.

All boys then played in trees as a matter of course, as did my younger sister, Valerie, and her friend. When the east wind blew with great force through the Columbia River gorge, a frequent occurrence, we would climb some lofty, well-limbed firs that grew on a hill and take the full blast of the wind. Right up in the tops we'd be, where the trunk was a mere sapling. There the wind would fling the boughs about and we'd hang on tight. In the big puffs my sister would scream and I'd sing a song that seemed somehow to fit the occasion, though now I can see no connection. The song was called "Thy Knight." This knight sat in his armor on his horse by a castle and sang to a very virgin lady in a high window: "Thy sentinel am I. I guard thee night and day. The wind and rain both rage in vain; my th-o-u-g-h-t-s are a-a-l-l-l of thee."

Between gusts we would snicker about the knight from up there in the trees. We'd wonder if his armor were rusting. We'd laugh as the gusts swung our trees way over and the boughs slapped us in the face. "A knight is a canned man," my sister would screech as we were buffeted about.

My friends Rolland and Newton Maddox and our dog, Sport, made the next seven years so brimful as to defy description. There were the two tracts of timber nearby and a boy's dream of a swamp with springs and, at the lower end, a long deep pond and a bit farther a small lake. A boyhood so accoutered and furnished with bosom companions and a dog—what more could a fellow want?

The Maddox boys lived halfway between the swamp and our house in a cottage on an acre of rich ground. Their father had surrounded the house with every kind of tree and bush and around that had created a vineyard and a small orchard. He planted as if intent on another Eden, and for the Maddox children and myself it undoubtedly was.

There we played a fiendish croquet, hoed the garden, climbed the maples and firs, and in autumn devoured bunches of grapes and apples without end. Elizabeth, their small, slender sister, wanted to be on our team, and to be more like a boy wore a truculent look when with us that, if strange boys came around, turned into the most baleful scowl possible.

We attended the same church and weren't allowed to swear or play tops or marbles for keeps because our parents said it was gambling. I was full of wild schemes that Rolland, a little older than I, brought practicality to.

One was the construction of a traveling clubhouse—a sort of lightweight shed built on two slender poles that four boys could carry like a palanquin. It had a carpeted floor, pockets in the sides that held food, cooking utensils, a hatchet, and pitchy kindling, and an overhanging roof that protected the opening in front. Using money earned selling old bottles, we had bought the thin boards needed to make it for a pittance from an old man who garnered them from the mills in the district.

There were six of us involved, and when school let out at noon four boys would grab the long handles and race away to some wooded place or field, set it down, and start a fire under the overhang. The other two would bring up the rear, carrying a large roll of discarded chicken-wire fencing on a pole between them. This we put up to make a barricade around our encampment in case an opposing force should attack.

Rain or snow, with one boy standing guard, five of us would cram into the little shed beneath the overhang and, crouching over our campfire, gulp down the smoky meats or the hot canned beans we had cooked along with the cookies or fruit that were in our lunch boxes. Then we would rush the clubhouse back to school before the bell rang.

From the time I was ten until I was seventeen I also did the chores. Twice

At the edge of a Pacific Northwest town in the early twentieth century. (Courtesy California State Library, Sacramento)

our house won the best-kept-place award in an extensive district. We had one hundred rosebushes pruned high on neat stems, a great block of dahlias, another of gladiolas, and a long, long border eight feet wide that was always a blaze of harmonious color. There were eight fruit trees, rows of berry bushes, a small hothouse, chicken house, pigeon house, and a large garden.

Chores! Once a week the basement floor had to be scrubbed and mopped dry, the same with the chicken-house floor and its appurtenances, and the pigeon house and the chipmunk cage. The area between the sidewalk and the curb had to be without a blade of grass and arise in a perfect semicircular curve on which stood the single stems of rosebushes.

I painted the house, hoed the garden, oiled the roof, hoed the garden some more, mowed the lawn, and polished the damned place until it looked unreal. If a job was skimped on in any way and found so on inspection, I got a good licking. The various neighbors offered to bring the Cruelty to Children people out to take a hand, but I refused. I loved my honest, rather shallow father. Saturday afternoons and Sundays were mine if all my work was done and favorably inspected Friday night. Then he would give me a few dimes for my needs and the fare back from as far as I could wander into the countryside or mountains. I would have my chores done and get away before anyone knew it. Monday, Tuesday, and Wednesday I tore into the work on my list of weekly jobs.

The Maddox boys and I often talked about building a log cabin and finding a place to erect it where progress wouldn't threaten it. Progress! When a group of people and horses—slovenly dressed women, a trailing of toddlers, men with great drooping mustaches, masters of the teams of horses—suddenly appeared somewhere with their tents and trappings we knew what it meant. With their wagons and equipment they would set up camp in a woods haven of ours: the place where we trapped squirrels, the leafy tangle where we picked buckets of blackberries or the place where we got the long, almost taperless poles for which we and our families had a hundred uses. Whoever owned the land they were camped on was going to have streets graded and sidewalks put through and would sell some lots.

Before such activity came, there were paths wandering through the woods between scattered houses. Many had been made by cows ranging for grass in the little clearings. Some were old deer trails of a more distant past, but to me, a boy running through them, they were a secret delight. So we dreaded the teamsters' changes on our vast playground but, in spite of it, admired their gypsy ways.

Each man had a team or two of draft horses; their movements were slow and swaggering. They were curt with whoever addressed them, for they had been annoyed countless times by the remarks of huffy people who demanded: "What do you think you're doing here anyway?" As the producers of change, they were at odds with the people who had "settled in" and wanted to keep it the way it was. Their paths wandered through the woods on what they considered to be public land.

World War I was ravaging Europe. The Spanish influenza was killing more people than the war and because of it our schools were closed. We kids were free to do as we pleased. The appearance of the gypsylike purveyors of change made us realize that we'd better get our log cabin up before it was too late. We did.

First, though, we dug a cave. Such a cave as, I believe, boys have never dug before. We were joined by Kingsley Harris and his brother, and the five of us with our carts made the dirt fly.

Near the Maddox place was a ravine with no houses close by. The sides of the ravine were clothed with a dense stand of medium-size firs. It seemed to be a splendid place to make a cave. I recall Rolland's unhappiness about the wild idea and his need to bring common sense to my plan.

We dug into the side of the ravine, throwing the dirt—the tailings really—

down the gully. By the end of the second day we had tunneled in about six feet. From this entrance tunnel we went at an angle for eight feet, then turned and went on in a northeasterly direction past a toolroom where our carts and shovels were stored, on about twenty-five feet to the main room, thirteen feet in diameter and thirteen feet to the peaked ceiling. Here we dug six throne seats into the walls. We traveled through all this with our small carts, removing the dirt as we dug at the face of the tunnel.

During this time I was sleeping in a tent with a fly over it. There was a floor in it about a foot above ground. It was believed in those days that lots of fresh air was extremely important to health in general. Tuberculosis was feared, and many people were battling it. Windows were flung wide in all bedrooms, and not a few people slept in tents. It was assumed that, if you slept in one long enough, it would make a robust athlete of you.

My parents, being Christian Scientists, wouldn't contaminate us with *materia medica* (cough drops, aspirin, or even salt water, if it were to be used as a gargle). But deep breathing, she didn't say anything about that. She being our leader, Mary Baker Eddy. So I got the tent. What freedom!

To curb any possible nocturnal romps, my parents had me undress in my bedroom, come downstairs in my nightgown, and kiss them good-night on my way out. Before I left the bedroom, however, I threw some clothes out the window, soon recovered them, and was free to prowl to Kingsley's house. From their barnyard I got a long ladder that I reared up over the room where their father slept to theirs above, and, cautiously, quietly, down would come Kingsley and his brother. Rolland and Newton's bedroom on the ground floor presented no problem, and we'd get in a three-hour dig. This was after Mr. Maddox found the cave and, seeing the dangers of a cave-in, informed Kingsley's parents and mine, and we were forbidden to go near it.

The tent house had another use for me, for the year before I had by accident discovered the calisthenic and cataclysmic act of masturbation, then known as self-abuse. It was strange; I knew little else about sex. I was in a fright about the almost certain possibility that my ears would wilt and fall off if I did it—masturbate. Still, I thought, I hadn't much choice, for if I didn't do it, utterly voluptuous wet dreams assailed me about every other night, and it was well-known in provincial circles that debility and death were the result of losing this—The Life Force.

So when I couldn't sleep and that troublesome organ was awake, too, I would jump out of bed, take off my nightgown and swing on the horizontal bar I had put outside for this purpose. I did the kip and swung from my knees and from my heels and did chin-ups until I was exhausted. Upon returning to bed, if we still couldn't sleep I would jump out, hastily put on clothes and run and walk through the sleeping suburbs to Mount Scott, four miles away. I'd climb a fire-blighted snag and up there, sitting on a limb stub, sing my favorite hymns and finally, late in the night, come down and walk back shriven of desire. But when it was raining heavily, which was often the case, well, what could a poor boy do?

We boys of the time were indeed brave, for with disfiguration and death staring us in the face we skipped blithely about, avoiding what we were told.

I admired my grandmother's hired men, several of them, as they drifted through. Theirs was a simple way of living. Their belongings consisted of only a spare shirt, extra socks, bandanna, and razor, and I liked their lack of interest in the baits of progress. It appealed to my growing distaste for the excess clutter of belongings. I was beginning to think independently; I decided I would be a hired man myself, and the sooner the better.

Early that summer my parents allowed me to become a strawberry picker on a farm high on Underwood Mountain, across the Columbia from the Hood River valley. I was allowed to go with Mrs. Isley, the adoptive mother of Aust, a boy in my class at school. The deciding element in my getting away from

*A fearsome-looking
Rice at age fourteen or
fifteen. (From the Rice
family collection)*

home was that Mrs. Isley belonged to our church. SHE WAS C.S. This qualified her in every direction.

I slipped away from our tents before Mrs. Isley and the sun were up and without the small sum owed me by the farmer for my labor in his strawberry fields. Adventure beckoned. Across the great river the valley lay and inveigled me to come and be a hired man in its orchards. After all I was fifteen, wasn't I? Time was a-wasting.

I had grown almost a head taller in the last couple of years and my voice had changed. Sadly my mother admitted that her secret hope, that I would be a famous tenor, was doomed.

I marched on down the mountain with the big pack Uncle Steve had given me, stuffed with camping gear. Odd! Here I was at last free to do as I pleased and I felt awful. My head was beginning to ache and my neck hurt. It's the pack, I told myself. I'm not used to it yet.

The sun was beginning to warm the land when I reached Underwood. I bought a can of pilchards in tomato sauce and some crackers to eat. Still under my pack, I strolled out to see when the boat for Hood River was due. It was on the point of leaving, but they held onto the dock, being already cast off, until I got aboard.

The ferry was a small double-ended fish boat. It rollicked over the waves and I felt queasy. My neck felt hot under my hands. From the boat I stumbled into a grove of cottonwoods by the river's edge and flopped to the sand and vomited. I vaguely noticed that I was in a hobo hangout. I fell asleep.

With the time past noon I awoke from an unsettling dream. As the sun beat down upon me I staggered up and dragged my pack into the shade. I went over to a couple of bums nearby and asked where I could get a drink of water. They pointed to a spring a few feet from where they sat.

I got out my cup and bailed up some of it, but with a sudden shock realized I couldn't swallow the water and that my throat was burning. What was wrong?

I spit out the water and touched my neck. Golly! It felt funny and hot.

An old, wizened bo had gotten up and stepped over to me. "What's the matter, kiddo?" he asked. "You sick?"

Through bleary eyes I regarded him. After a time I muttered, "Yes, guess that's so."

"Here," he said, "hold your head up. Lemme look at you." He made a quick perusal of my face. "Yep, you're sick all right. You got the mumps. Hey," he remarked to another guy, "see his jaws? The left one is all swole. See it?"

"How could I miss it," the other man said. "Listen! I hear her comin'. Let's get down to the tracks!"

The old man put his hand on my forehead. "Hell, kid," he said, "you got a hundred and four fever or I ain't never been around. Get down a lot of water and lay in the shade. Couple days you'll be all right." He hurried after his companion.

He was right. I lay on my blankets by the spring, hazy with fever. After a couple of days the swelling subsided. No one touched my pack as I lay there. Some even brought me water in my cup. Finally I opened the can of big sardines and got them down. Rough! The crackers were easier soaked in water. I was weak and hungry and, as reaching into my pockets proved, I was also broke.

I got my pack on and headed for the road that led into the orchard country, resting often. I figured it out at twelve rests per mile, but I kept coming on. At last I saw a man irrigating his orchard. Weakly I swaggered over to him.

"How about a hired man to help you with that?" I said, then rested. That was all I had for the moment.

He allowed me a day to regain my strength and I got along fine working there for the next two weeks. I liked my employer and his wife. Then I was asked to irrigate several acres of apple trees while the couple were away for the day, and when the job was completed, as a special bonus to these kind people, I also irrigated a small block of pear trees. It took a lot of doing and I was proud of my accomplishment. He fired me at once, for any one of several possible reasons.

I decided to look for work up under the lofty snows of Mount Adams in a tiny village named Laurel, where some distant relatives were said to live. I made the trip in a four-horse stage. The horses, half-broken cayuses of many colors, were seldom allowed to walk. About halfway there a band of wild horses came dashing through the scattered pines and accompanied us on both sides as we tore along. Then they left us, angling away from the road into some hills. The stage driver was able to keep our four from going with them by his expertise with the reins. It was an uncertain but, to me, exciting moment, this separation of the wild from the tamed, a matter of a slight diversion of goals, for the wild horses did seem to have one.

I sat behind the driver and his partner, amid baggage piled on top of the stage. They talked incessantly of their sexual conquests and of girls. I got the picture that girls in this part of the country were lush and eager, and that in darkness one of the village schoolhouse's steps was the best place for such

The afternoon stages arrive at a California lumber camp in 1910. Note the automobile in the center of the photo. (Courtesy California State Library, Sacramento)

Lumberjacks take time out for a midday meal break.
(Courtesy California State Library, Sacramento)

trystings. I learned more about sex while traveling to Laurel than I ever knew existed. I stepped off the stage at my destination amazed with this new outlook on things. I fitted it in with Tennyson's view of what went on at King Arthur's court.

I soon found a job as an off-bearer from a band saw in a box-shook mill. The boss grinned at me as I went to work. "Think you can cut it, fella?" he said.

"Fella," he said, not kid. People were beginning to see how it was. A guy out on his own and getting ready to take a man's job shouldn't be called a kid anymore.

I did "cut it," as he said, though I was startled by the pace they set. Then a mill hand toppled a stack of shook down on me, and gashes in my right arm removed me from the roster of working stiffs. I returned home with a paycheck and wounds, gotten while attendant to the lordly band saw.

And, yes, the boss did call me "fella" once more, and told me he'd have a job waiting for me next summer.

WALLACE STEGNER

Wally Stegner lives with Mary, his wife of fifty-five years, in the hills above Los Altos, California, not far from Stanford University, where he taught creative writing for so many years. I met him one summer day in Anaheim, 350 miles to the south, where the nation's booksellers had gathered to do their annual business and to honor the current stars of the American literary scene. He had been asked by his publisher to come, he said, to help draw attention to his latest novel, *Crossing to Safety,* which would be appearing in paperback soon.

It isn't the sort of thing that comes easily to Stegner, this glad greeting of a curious public. Even after fifty-two years as a writer and some twenty-eight published books, he is obviously a private man, made uncomfortable by the spotlight. Nevertheless, that day he did everything that was asked of him: trudging dutifully through the crowded aisles of the Anaheim Convention Center to stand and be photographed beneath the dust-jacket blowup of his novel; sitting as guest of honor at a luncheon gathering for the nation's book reviewers and trying without much success to look at ease (at least he didn't have to speak—right up to the end he had feared that he might); peering out across a high table in a sort of rogues' lineup of available authors, prepared to sign autograph after autograph for an unending row of fans.

In the book *Conversations with Wallace Stegner,* written with Richard W. Etulain and published by the University of Utah Press a few years ago, Stegner

Wallace Stegner. (Photo by Joe Backes)

made the point that all lives dedicated to cultural achievement are certainly not equal. "If you start pretty much at the bottom, at some Neanderthal homestead in Saskatchewan," he had said with conviction, having started exactly there, "you have to try to come up the whole way in one lifetime, to something like the peak of your civilization, whatever that may be. It's demoralizing." So much, then, for the Groton and Exeter graduates scrawling their signatures one table on either side of him, the sons and granddaughters of inherited taste who had been able to go chasing after culture, so to speak, with a running start. He himself, he is quick to remind you, was first of all a barefoot farm boy. As in dirt farm, never mind your waves of grain and sturdy, corn-filled silos; his father went bust so many times trying merely to scratch life from a dusty land that the word ceased to have meaning anymore. Neither of his parents had attended school beyond the eighth grade. And while he himself, in classic overachiever fashion, not only far surpassed that and went on to earn his college diploma, then a master's degree and even a doctorate, and went on after that to teach for almost forty years at fine schools such as Stanford and Harvard and the American Academy in Rome, it was always a far stretch and he never quite got over it. Looking back he could see even now that it was a long, long way he had finally come.

These things were on his mind that day in Anaheim, maybe because the surroundings themselves gave rise to another obvious thought: that this, right now, could well be the other end of that lifetime journey he had discussed with Etulain as well—the peak, the final result of his years of cultural striving. His has been a rather unorthodox literary career, with several relatively early triumphs, followed by years of frustration, capped by a string of coveted honors received at an age when most serious writers are living on the memories of past glories. Now, at eighty, he could look around at last and see from the reactions of others that his time as a literary presence on the American scene had certainly arrived.

"Mister Stegner, I don't like to rank books," enthused an elderly, bearded man at the front of the autograph line, "but if I had to list my top five, your *Crossing to Safety* and *Angle of Repose* would have to be among them."

"Well good," replied Stegner, obviously pleased. "I wish there were more like you."

It all began with a novella titled *Remembering Laughter,* about farm life in rural Iowa, which Stegner wrote as a young college English instructor in Salt Lake City shortly after his marriage to Mary. It won the Little, Brown novelette contest of 1937—which had been the idea to begin with; he had set to work with the goal of winning it. With the $2,500 prize money he quit teaching and the couple bicycled around France and England for the summer. It was great fun, but little more really than a holiday from life's more sober responsibilities, and Stegner knew it. "It never occurred to me then that anybody could actually make a living from writing," he says, "so I didn't think of giving up my teaching career." That fall he accepted a position at the University of Wisconsin, and moved on to Harvard two years later.

As it turned out, it was a wise career choice; his next four published books—three novels, *The Potter's House, On a Darkling Plain,* and *Fire and Ice,* and a nonfiction book, *Mormon Country*—hardly set the publishing world on fire.

In 1943, however, came another novel, *The Big Rock Candy Mountain,* and for the first time Stegner had not only a literary success but a commercial best-seller as well. A family chronicle set in the vastness of the American West, the novel featured one Bo Mason, a character obviously based upon Stegner's footloose father, and his compulsive quest to find success even at the expense of family harmony.

On the strength of his burgeoning reputation, Stegner accepted a year-long assignment from *Look* magazine to travel and work on the text for a book to be called *One Nation,* a look at racial prejudice in wartime America.

Wallace Stegner.
(Photo by Joe Backes)

When that project was finished, rather than return to Harvard as a lowly assistant professor he accepted an offer at Stanford, with the rank of full professor.

It was, Stegner says now, an idyllic time. "I arrived just as the GI students were flooding back—the best students and the most motivated that any professor ever had." In the following years he would teach such future literary luminaries as Thomas McGuane, Edward Abbey, Scott Momaday, Tillie Olsen, Robert Stone, Larry McMurtry, Ernest Gaines, Max Apple, Ken Kesey, and countless others; the list could go on and on. He was suddenly, without doubt, the most respected—and certainly the most visible—writing teacher in America. On the side, meanwhile, he became the West Coast editor of Houghton Mifflin and brought to that house, among other books, Tom Heggen's wildly successful *Mister Roberts.* He served briefly as assistant to the U.S. Secretary of the Interior, became chairman of the National Parks Advisory Board, was editor of *American West* magazine.

But his own writing, while it continued to appear at its old, furious rate, seemed to go into a troubling decline. In 1950 his *The Preacher and the Slave* was published, a historical novel based on the life of Joe Hill, the enigmatic union leader who was executed for murder in Utah, and when the critics turned their backs on it—or worse yet, seemed to completely miss its point—Stegner in disgust abandoned book-length fiction altogether for ten years. Instead, he turned to such projects as *Beyond the Hundredth Meridian,* a biography of early Western geologist-explorer John Wesley Powell; *Wolf Willow,* a combination autobiography-history-anthology dealing with his early Saskatchewan days, and two collections of short stories. Only in 1961, with *A Shooting Star,* did he publish another novel, and then it was of a decidedly different kind than any he had done before—set in the modern era, located in trendy, upper-class California, told from a woman's point of view. Several others in the same vein followed.

The decade of the 1970s provided, finally, a break with all that. First of all, it ended for good his academic career.

"I didn't really retire from Stanford, you see. I resigned. That was in 1971. After the turmoil of the late sixties, I had become sick and tired of all the disruptions that were making teaching really quite impossible.

I looked at myself and my age, which was then sixty-two, and I realized I had only so many years left. And I asked myself why I was wasting it this way. I had better things to do. So I quit, after twenty-six years there. I gave up whatever claim I might have had on retirement benefits and the like and just left.

"For years after that, whenever the university's officials talked to alumni groups about Stanford's excellent faculty privileges, they would cite me as an example of someone who was able to take advantage of the early retirement program when it came about. But it wasn't true. I asked for and got nothing at all."

He turned, at last, to full-time writing, with the aid of a six-book contract negotiated by his agent that provided him with some degree of financial security. And within a year it proved to be, once more, the wise career choice: He won the Pulitzer Prize for his very next novel, *Angle of Repose.* Five years later he added the National Book Award for *The Spectator Bird,* and in 1980 he received the Robert Kirsch Award, given by the *Los Angeles Times* for outstanding lifetime achievement by a Western writer.

Not bad for an old farm boy.

At the Viking/Penguin booth on the convention floor, publisher types were singing his praises to thousands of bookstore owners beneath a sign proclaiming him ONE OF AMERICA'S FOREMOST AUTHORS. Fellow writers were coming by to greet him. Not really too bad at all.

C.B., 1988

A rancher's wife be-neath a row of shade trees in the front yard of her Utah home. (Courtesy Special Collections, University of Utah Library)

Finding the Place

I had no understanding of it while it was happening, did not comprehend either my deprivations or my advantages until acquaintance with other regions and older cultures began to define for me the terms of my identity, but from February 1909, when I was born on my grandfather's farm near Lake Mills, Iowa, to September 1930, when I boarded a bus in Salt Lake City to go "back East" to graduate school in Iowa, all the places I knew were Western: North Dakota wheat towns, Washington logging camps, Saskatchewan prairie hamlets and homesteads, and the cities of Seattle, Great Falls, Salt Lake, Hollywood, and Reno, with a lot of country seen on the fly between them.

My father was a boomer, a gambler, a rainbow-chaser, as footloose as a tumbleweed in a windstorm. My mother was always hopefully, hopelessly, trying to nest. I used to think that I was shaped by motion, but I find on thinking it over that what most conditioned me was the two places where we stayed long enough to put down roots and grow associations and memories and friends and a degree of self-confidence.

Nevertheless, the characteristic Western migratoriness cannot be disregarded. Growing up culturally malnourished, I hunted the Big Rock Candy Mountain as hungrily as ever my father did, but it was a mountain of a different kind. He wanted to make a killing and end up on Easy Street. I wanted to move back into the civilization I felt I was constantly being dragged away from. So my wheels didn't stop rolling until at the age of thirty-six, after several years of graduate school in Iowa and California, and a decade of teaching in Illinois, Utah, Wisconsin, and Massachusetts, I arrived with my wife and son at Stanford and the house in the Coast Range foothills, within sight of the last sunsets on the continent, where we have lived ever since. Teaching at Harvard, which should have gratified my greatest ambition, I found that I couldn't wait to get back West.

The years since 1945 have been, in the main, happy, contented, and reasonably productive ones, but like all busy years, they tend to blur and flow together. It is the years when the West was still pretty young and I was even younger, the years when a full round of the seasons was a seventh or an eighth of my life instead of a seventieth or an eightieth, that are indelible.

My first five years were constant motion, and what I retain of them is no more than flits and flashes, images on a broken film flapping through the projector: rare sun on the roof of our tent in the deep woods that are now Redmond, Washington; the musty, buttery odor of the bread crusts distributed from a dishpan at midmorning in the Seattle orphanage where my desperate mother stashed my brother and me for a while; the foreign smells and foreign sounds of my grandfather's Norwegian-speaking house in Lake Mills when we retreated there in the winter of 1913; the bare benches and varnished wainscots of the railroad station in Weyburn, on the Canadian border, with stern men in red coats staring down from the walls.

Those are preliminaries. The real film begins in the summer of 1914 in the raw new nontown of Eastend, Saskatchewan, where the Frenchman Creek flows out of the Cypress Hills. That was the first place in my life where we lived for more than a few months. I was five when we arrived, eleven when we left. The years when I watched that town get born were the shaping years of my life. I have never forgotten a detail of them.

Cecil, left, and Wally Stegner engage in a spectacular boat race in a Seattle studio portrait in 1913. (From the Stegner family collection)

Eastend when we arrived was the Z-X ranch house and a boardinghouse for the crews building the grade for a branch line down from Swift Current. Its history, which none of us knew, was short and violent. Métis winterers had not ventured into the dark and bloody hills, disputed ground among the tribes, until 1867. In 1869 the Hudson's Bay Company built a post on Chimney Coulee that lasted only one season before it was destroyed by the Blackfeet. In the 1870s the Mounties built a patrol post to keep an eye on the Sioux and Nez Percés who had fled north of the line after the Indian wars. And in the 1880s cattle began coming in from Montana, and spread over all that range for twenty years. The terrible winter of 1906–7 put most of the outfits out of business. The Z-X was a remnant survivor. Out of it we and a dozen other families carved a townsite.

Within a few weeks, when the rails were laid, the town grew by some derailed boxcars, old Pullmans, and a superannuated dining car. We lived the first winter in the dining car, considered pretty classy. Later we lived in a rented shack. After about two years, my father built a house and a small barn down in the west end, on the river.

The first year was a chaos of experiences, good and bad. I caught lice from the half-Indian kids I played with, and was fiercely shampooed with kerosene. I learned dirty words and dirty songs from the children of construction workers and from the Z-X cowpunchers. With others, I was induced to ride calves and engage in "shit fights" with wet cow manure in the Z-X corrals. Then or later I learned to dog-paddle, first in the irrigation ditch, later in the river, and I fished for suckers in the deep holes of the bends, and followed trails through willows that felt like authentic wilderness. Then or later we put .22 cartridges or blasting caps on the tracks ahead of approaching handcars or speeders, and once we got satisfactorily chased by gandy dancers. Around Christmas we all watched the first soldiers go off to the war, and then and afterward we had trouble with some Canadian kids who said the United States was too yellow to fight. They had a song for us:

Here's to the American eagle
He flies over mountain and ditch
But we don't want the turd of your goddamn bird
You American son of a bitch

My brother, who was big for his age, and tough, fought every kid his size, and some bigger, in defense of America's honor. But we were ashamed, and we got an instructive taste of how it felt to be disliked for tribal affiliations that we hadn't really known we had.

The town grew around us, and incorporated us, and became our familiar territory: Main Street with its plank sidewalks, its drug and grocery and hardware stores, its Pastime theater, its lumberyard, its hotel and bank; Millionaire Row with its four or five bungalows with sweet peas and nasturtiums in their yards; Poverty Flat, where the two Chinese and some métis had shacks.

The people we knew were of many kinds: métis left over from the fur-trade days, Texas and Montana cowpunchers left over from the cattle period, and a stew of new immigrants, Ontario men, cockneys fresh from another East End, Scandinavians moving up the migration route from the Dakotas to the Northwest, and a few Jews, a Syrian family, a couple of Chinese, a Greek. Mark Twain, confronted by a colorful character, used to say, "I know him—knew him on the river." I could say, about as legitimately, "I know him—knew him in Eastend." A young frontier gathers every sort of migrant, hope-chaser, roughneck, trickster, incompetent, misfit, and failure. All kinds passed through our town, and some stayed, or were stuck.

Our doctor was a drifter and a drunk who finally died of eating Canned Heat. Our dentist came through only once a year, and in a week did more harm than an ordinary dentist could have done in a decade. Religiously we were served by a shack-chapel and an itinerant priest for the métis, and a Presbyterian church with resident pastor for everybody else. The Scandinavians, Germans, Ontario men, Englishmen, and run-of-the-mine Americans, even the Syrian grocer and his family, became Presbyterians because that was where the only social action was. The Jewish butcher, the cowpunchers, the two Chinese who ran the restaurant, and the Greek who took it over from them—all without families—remained refractory and unassimilable.

When we arrived, and for a couple of years thereafter, the Frenchman River still had beaver, muskrats, mink, weasels, sandhill cranes; in the willow breaks were big populations of cottontails and snowshoe hares preyed on by coyotes and lynxes. On the long, mainly roadless way to the homestead down on the Montana line—two days by lumber wagon with the cow tied behind, one day by Democrat, seven or eight excruciating hours by Model T—we passed sloughs swarming with nesting ducks. On the homestead itself, dry country far from any slough, it was all flickertails, prairie dogs, badgers, black-footed ferrets, coyotes, gopher snakes, and hawks. That prairie, totally un-suited to be plowed up, was hawk heaven. I find now, decades later when it has all been returned to grass, that ornithologists come from far-off universities to study ferruginous hawks there. I never knew their species name, but I knew their look in the sky or on a fence post, and more than once one fell out of the empty blue to strike a pullet in the yard within a few yards of me.

We plowed our first field, and dammed our coulee, and built our shack, in the summer of 1915, and thereafter we spent the summers on the home-stead, the winters in town. It was an uneven division, for in that latitude a wheat crop, from seed time to harvest, took only about three months. But either on the prairie or in town we were only a step from the wild, and we wavered between the pleasure it was to be part of it and the misguided conviction we had that we must destroy it in our own interest. There are two things that growing up in the West, on a belated frontier, gave me: an acquaintance with the wild and wild creatures, and guilt for my part in their destruction.

I was a sickly child, but hardly a tame one. Like all the boys I knew, I had

*Some Z-X riders in Eastend, around 1910, and the stag hound that
Stegner used as the model for Puma in his story "Genesis." The flume
carried the Z-X irrigation ditch. (From the Stegner family collection)*

a gun, and used it, from the age of eight or nine. We shot at anything that
moved, we killed everything not domesticated or protected. In winter we
trapped the small fur-bearers of the river bottoms, in summer my brother and
I spent hours of every day trapping, shooting, snaring, poisoning, or drowning
out the gophers that gathered to our wheat and to the dependable water of
our "rezavoy." We poisoned out the prairie dogs, and incidentally did in the
black-footed ferrets that lived on them—ferrets that now are the rarest North
American mammals. We didn't even know they were ferrets: We called them

*A sheepherder's son displays the string of fish he has
caught in a pond in the Western desert, 1907. (Courtesy
Special Collections, University of Utah Library)*

big weasels. But we killed them as we killed everything else. Once I speared one with a pitchfork in the chicken house, and was sickened by its ferocious vitality, dismayed by how hard the wild died. I had the same feeling when I caught a badger in a gopher trap. I would gladly enough have let him loose, but he was too fierce, and lunged at me too savagely, and in the end I had to stone him to death.

Nobody could have been more brainlessly and immorally destructive. And yet there was love there, too. We took delight in knowing the animals we killed, our pets were all captives from the wild—burrowing owls, magpies, a coyote pup, a ferret that I caught in a trap and kept in a screened beer case and fed with live gophers. One of the first short stories I ever wrote, one called "Bugle Song" that was later incorporated into *The Big Rock Candy Mountain,* was a moment from that tranced, murderous summer season when I went from poetry and daydreaming to killing and back to daydreaming. "Bugle Song" is an idyll counterweighted by death.

Our neighbors were few and miles away, most of them across the line in Montana. For two weeks at a time we might see no one but ourselves; and when our isolation was broken, it was generally broken by a lonesome Swede home-steader who came over, ostensibly to buy eggs, but more probably to hear the sound of a human voice. We welcomed him. We were as hungry for the sound of a voice as he was.

I am somewhat skeptical of the fabled Western self-reliance, because as I knew it the West was a place where one depended on neighbors, and had to give as well as get. In any trouble, I ran, or rode one of the horses, four or five miles to get Tom Larson or Ole Telepo or someone else to help. They came to us the same way. And yet there is something about living in big empty space, under a great sky that is alternately serene and furious, exposed to intolerable sun from four in the morning till nine at night, and to a wind that never seems to rest—there is something in that big country that tells an individual not only how small he is but also tells him *who* he is. I have never understood people with identity problems. Any time I lay awake at night and heard the wind in the screens and saw the moon ride up in the sky, or sat reading in the shade of the shack and heard the wind moan and mourn around the corners, or slept out under the wagon and heard it searching among the spokes of the wheels, I knew well enough who I was, even if I *didn't* matter. As surely as any pullet in the yard, I was a target, and I had better respect what had me in its sights.

I never came out to the homestead in June without anticipation and delight. I never returned to town in September without a surge of joy—back to safety and shelter, back to the river and the willow breaks, back to friends, games, Sunday-school parties, back to school, where I could shine.

It is a common notion that children reared in lonely or isolated places yearn for the color and action and excitement and stimulation of gaudier places. Adolescents, maybe; not children of the age I was, in the place where I lived. Everything I knew was right around me, and it was enough.

We studied geography and history in school, but those subjects never suggested to me that I was deprived. I knew little history, no architecture, no art, only the crudest of music, but I never missed them. We learned a lot of poetry, and got to "speak pieces" at school or church or town celebrations, and I read everything that fell into my hands, but it never occurred to me to make a conscious effort to expand my horizons. I lived contentedly at the center of my primitive culture, soaked in its folklore, committed to its harsh code of conduct even when I despaired of living up to it, and I was full to the eyes with its physical, sensuous beauty, and submissive to its brutal weathers, and familiar, in ridicule or respect, with its drunken cowboys and its ranting newspaper editors and its limp English barristers incapable of a syllable more complex than "Haw!" I was at home, and content, and I might have lived there for a long time, perhaps forever, and become a wheat farmer or a local schoolteacher with a literary streak and a taste for local lore.

But my father's luck took care of that. We had had a big 1915 crop, forty bushels to the acre at nearly three dollars a bushel. That so exploded the optimistic synapses of his brain that in 1916 he plowed and seeded another sixty acres besides the forty of his first field. 1916 was very wet. Water stood all summer in the burn-cuts, the wheat developed rust, the crop was small and of poor quality. Very well. Next year, then, with more acreage. Next year, 1917, we got burned out by hot winds. 1918, then, with more acreage still. A system—double when you lose! 1918 we got burned out again. Okay, 1919. 1919 it hardly rained at all, the wheat had hardly sprouted before it withered, the fields were dust before mid-July. In 1920 my father decided what some other families had already decided, and we gave up our pretense of being Canadians and moved to Montana.

In *The Big Rock Candy Mountain* there is a chapter, made out of a short story called "The Colt," that reports our leaving Eastend, and the desolation of young Bruce Mason, who is of course myself, when they drive past the dump on the way out of town and he sees the skinned body of his crippled colt, the iron braces still on its front legs, thrown on the dump. He had thought the colt was going to be cared for at a ranch downriver, and what he saw on the dump made him pull a blanket over his head and bawl.

That is not quite the way we left. I pulled a blanket over my head and bawled, all right; and I had a crippled colt, and he ended up on that dump, skinned for his three-dollar hide. But in the story I was just finding justifications for my distress. My colt had been killed and skinned the year before. All I was bawling about as we left was the mere leaving. I realized, in the very thrill of moving, that I was leaving behind my friends, the river's wild-rose bars and cutbank bends, the secret hideouts in the brush, Chimney Coulee's berry patches, the sound of water running under the sagging snowbanks in May, the Chinook winds with their fierce blizzardy sound and their touch as warm as milk—everything I had intimately known, everything I was.

I left Saskatchewan mourning what I had left behind and scared of what we were going toward, and one look at my mother told me she was feeling the same way. My father and brother were leaning out of the car, exhilarated by how the fence posts flew by on the smooth dirt road along the South Bench bounding the river valley. They leaned and watched the roadside as if they were afraid Great Falls might flash by at any second, and they might miss it. But I was at heart a nester, like my mother; I loved the place I was losing, the place that my living had worn smooth.

Great Falls was not a really significant part of my boyhood; it was a transition, a roadside stop, between Eastend and Salt Lake City, the two locations where I felt like a placed and not a displaced person. Nevertheless it couldn't help enlarging me, sometimes bitterly.

In my first day there I made the acquaintance of things I had read about but never seen: lawns, cement sidewalks, streetcars, streets with names, houses with numbers. I had never known anybody with a street address. Now I had one myself: 448 Fourth Avenue North. And in the house on Fourth Avenue North were other things I had never seen: hardwood floors that were wonderful to skate around on in stocking feet, a bathroom with a tub and running water, a flush toilet. It was incredible that only the day before, we had lived in a world of privies and washbasins and slop buckets. I grew vastly in my own estimation by what I was introduced to.

But I hung around the house, unwilling to risk meeting strange kids in the street, and my first day of school was a disaster.

In the flurry of our moving in, my mother had not been able to get me properly outfitted, and had to ask me, apologetically, if I minded going in my old clothes for the first day or two. I didn't mind. In fact, I had a fantasy of walking into this new school in my Canadian clothes and being a sensation, a frontiersman, a fellow from wild country. I had an orange sweater with a wide white stripe around the chest, something I had picked out myself from the T. Eaton catalog, and I wore my elk-hide moccasins, the standard footwear in Eastend until snow made the change to shoepacs necessary. On the way to school I practiced stalking, rising on my toes at each step, and I kept a taciturn half-sneer on my face, wanting to look as I imagined Daniel Boone might have looked while tracking a bear.

Unfortunately I was not six feet three, but four feet ten. My moccasins drew stares, my sweater laughter. *Hey, f'Gawd's sake, lookit what's comin', a Hampshire shoat. Hey, shoat, how'd you leave things down to the pigpen?* What compounded my outsider-ness was that I was two years ahead of myself in school, and at eleven was supposed to enter the eighth grade, where everybody else was at least thirteen or fourteen, and where there was one boy six feet high and in need of a shave.

I came late to Miss Temby's class and stood in the door, and a wave of laughter burst in my face. My ears on fire, I slunk to the seat Miss Temby pointed me to, and when she gave us, that very first day, a review test in geometry to see how much we had remembered over the summer, I remembered nothing, for geometry was a seventh-grade subject and I had skipped the seventh grade. By intuition and guesswork I managed a score of twelve out of a possible hundred.

That day left permanent scars on my self-confidence, though by working my head off I got to the top of Miss Temby's praise list before the year was over. When she assigned us ten lines of Joaquin Miller's "Columbus" to memorize, I memorized the whole poem, and recited it, as she exclaimed delightedly, "Without a single mistake!" She read aloud a couple of themes of mine (about Eastend, naturally), and by her praise may have given me an unnoticed shove toward a literary career.

But Miss Temby was the easiest part. My classmates, once they stopped staring or laughing, were too intent on their own pubescent affairs to notice a runt like me, except once when I split my thumb down to the first joint on a bench saw in shop, and bled all over the place, and bawled, not so much in pain as in outrage that the world could treat me so. And when my mother, learning how to drive, knocked a streetcar off its tracks and threw me against the front seat so hard it loosened my ribs and bent my new Eversharp pencil into a pretzel, even the notice in the paper managed to demean me. Listing the injuries, the reporter concluded that "the little boy, Wallace, was more frightened than hurt."

I was too little for school sports, which here were organized. I was too little for the Boy Scouts. I was too little to get a job as my brother did, tending the furnace for Charlie Russell, down the street, though in the spring I did get to mow the Russell lawn a couple of times. I was too little for anything, and I missed my friends. Psychiatrists nowadays would have explanations for why I reverted for a month or two to baby talk that drove my father wild.

By spring I was beginning to come out of it. I had a friend named Sloppy Thompson, I was able to join the Boy Scouts. We spent our weekends hiking down to the Giant Spring or Black Eagle Falls, or wading the rocky shallows above the Great Falls trying to catch carp in our bare hands. We hiked up the Missouri and swam a channel and camped on Third Island, we spent some spring Sundays on Sun River. Given time, I might have felt at home there as I had felt at home in Eastend. But by late June of 1921 we were on the road, heading south through the Little Belts and the Smith River valley, through Yellowstone and over Targhee Pass and through the Idaho towns, seeing the world, seeing the West, in a Hudson supersix with our camp beds and Stoll auto-tent on the running boards and a big grub box on the rear bumper.

On the road again, which was exciting, and less of a wrench than our departure from Eastend. But uprooted again, which made me uneasy.

I needn't have worried. Luck was with us. Though we saw a lot of the West in the years after 1921, and had short stays in Hollywood and Reno, we did our wandering from the fixed base of Salt Lake, or within the boundaries of the city. Between my twelfth and twenty-first years we must have lived in twenty different houses, and we never again became, as we had been in Eastend, a family with an attic and a growing accumulation of memorabilia and worn-out life gear and the artifacts of memory. Nevertheless we all, and my brother and I especially, began very soon to feel at home.

Salt Lake was then a city of a hundred thousand or so, small enough to know, and I learned it, on foot or by streetcar. It was a city built by Mormons, with a strong sense of family and community—something the Stegners and the people they had lived among were notably short of. My brother and I found, near the first house we moved into, a municipal playground, pronounced "muni-sipple," where he, a good athlete, was welcomed and even I was tolerated. We discovered the Mormon institution known as Mutual, for Mutual Improvement Association, which every Tuesday evening, in every ward house in Zion, provided everything from Boy Scout meetings and Bible classes to basketball leagues and teenage dances. There may have been a covert proselytizing motive in the welcome that the wards extended to strange gentile kids, but there was a lot of plain warmth and goodwill, too. I have never ceased to be grateful for what they gave us when what they gave mattered a great deal; and though I was never tempted to adopt their beliefs, I could never write about them, when it came to that, except as a friend. Their obsession with their history, too, made me aware that I had grown up entirely *without* history, and set me on the trail to construct some for myself.

What I wanted most, it seems to me now, was to belong, and Mormon institutions are made to order for belongers. Once in the Boy Scouts, I went

*Modern streetcars share Main Street with horse-drawn
wagons in this view of downtown Salt Lake City.
(C. R. Savage photo, courtesy Utah State Historical Society)*

up through the ranks to eagle like smoke up a chimney. I was a demon activist in school Latin clubs and drama societies (I played saucy bellhops and brattish boys). In my first year at East High School I was desolated when they wouldn't let me into ROTC, which was compulsory for all boys, because I didn't weigh a hundred pounds. Trying to work the angles, I tried out for the rifle team and made it, assuming that then they might let me in. Instead, they barred me from competing because I wasn't a member of ROTC. By overeating and muscling bricks I made it over the hundred-pound limit before the next year, and went through the ranks the way I had gone through the ranks of the Scouts—file-closer to sergeant, sergeant to first sergeant, first sergeant to second lieutenant, second lieutenant to first lieutenant. I had my moment of glory when, in Sam Browne belt, leather puttees, shoulder pips, and sword, I led a platoon down Main Street in the Decoration Day parade.

Then in my senior year, between the ages of fifteen and sixteen, I suddenly grew six inches. It was like a second graduation, more important to me than graduation from high school, and the beginning of the happiest years I ever knew or will know. Suddenly I was big enough to hold my own in sports. Suddenly I had friends who looked on me as an equal and not as a mascot. Suddenly, as a freshman in the University of Utah, I was playing on the freshman basketball squad and a little later on the tennis team. Suddenly I was being rushed by a fraternity and acquired brothers, and a secret grip, and a book of tong songs. Beatitude.

Toward the end of my freshman year I got a job working afternoons and Saturdays in a floor-covering store, at twenty-five cents an hour, and with financial independence achieved, began to date girls who a year earlier had looked over my head. The success of my transition from have-not to have was measured by my grades: straight A's as a freshman, straight B's as a sophomore. My companions included few intellectuals; most were jocks, card players, and beer drinkers. My long-term addiction to books, which had been

*Bathers—many in their hats—test the buoyancy of the
water in Great Salt Lake before the Pavilion in 1904.
(Courtesy Special Collections, University of Utah Library)*

intensified by access to the Carnegie Library on State Street, suffered. My literary ambitions, which had been stimulated by Vardis Fisher, my freshman English instructor, got shelved. I was almost glad that Fisher had left after my first year, and gone back to teach next to Tom Wolfe at NYU, for he had a caustic tongue and a great contempt for time wasters. Just the same, I wouldn't have traded my newly achieved life as an insider for an introduction to Clara Bow.

Then in September 1930, more by accident and the efforts of friends than through my own seeking, I was offered a teaching assistantship at the University of Iowa, and was uprooted again, this time alone. I suppose I learned more, and faster, during two years in Iowa City than in any two-year period of my life, and some of what I learned was about myself. I had always known, not always happily, *who* I was. Now I began to understand *what* I was. I was a Westerner.

Homesickness is a great teacher. It taught me, during an endless rainy fall, that I came from the arid lands, and liked where I came from. I was used to a dry clarity, a sharpness, in the air. I was used to horizons that either lifted into jagged ranges or rimmed the geometrical circle of the flat world. I was used to seeing a long way. I was used to earth colors—tan, rusty red, toned white— and the endless green of Iowa offended me. I was used to a sun that came up over the mountains and went down behind other mountains. I missed the color and smell of sagebrush, and the sight of bare ground.

What I was homesick for was not merely Salt Lake, a city in a valley between mountains, with the glint of the lake off westward, but for a whole region, a whole lifetime of acclimatization and expectation. Eastend was part of what I felt deprived of, and Great Falls, and the Great Basin desert that we had crossed many times on the way to Los Angeles or Reno or San Francisco. It was the red-rock country of the plateaus, where we had had a summer cottage on Fish Lake for several years, in the fir-fragrant air of eight thousand feet. It was the places where I had gone camping with my Boy Scout troop—Bryce and Zion and the Grand Canyon and Capitol Reef, and the Granddaddy Lakes wilderness in the Uintas. It was the whole West, and I began to realize how lucky I had been to see so much of it. I also began to realize how much it had had to do in the making of me.

Each of the three places I had lived in since the age of five had been close to wild country. Even Salt Lake, which had looked as vast as Rome to me, opened westward on empty desert, and eastward led into the mountains through seven major and many minor canyons. In my junior high and high school years we used to catch rides on Denver & Rio Grande freights at the mouth of Parley's Canyon, and ride up as far as Lamb's Canyon, and from there hike off into the remoter mountains, Holladay Park and other pockets. In Iowa City, during the long, intense, studious winter, I used to find myself thinking of the little slot of Hughes Canyon, between Big and Little Cottonwood, where in spring there were carpets of dogtooth violets.

I became a booster, talking up my home territory; and what is more significant, I began to write my life, and my life was all Western. I remember telling Stephen Vincent Benét, when he visited Iowa City, that I was going to write a three-decker novel, a peasant novel, about Saskatchewan. I didn't, but I wrote something comparable, *The Big Rock Candy Mountain.* And every story I tried to write evoked the smells and colors and horizons and air and people of the places where I had most lived.

That is essentially the whole story—I grew up Western, and the first time I lived outside the West I realized what that meant to me. The rest is documentation, detail.

At the end of that first Iowa year, I couldn't wait to get home, which turned out to be Reno instead of Salt Lake, but was at least in the dry West. The summer gave me the steam to get back to Iowa, which if the truth were told was enlarging me faster than the West ever had. The next school year I

Wally in a jaunty sailor cap, about age eighteen, at the Fish Lake cabin in Utah. (From the Stegner family collection)

enrolled at Berkeley, because my parents were living in California and my mother was ill. At the Fish Lake cottage the following summer I began the desolate duty of helping her die. When she did die, in November, we buried her in Salt Lake next to my brother, who had died of pneumonia two years earlier, and I went back to Iowa to finish my degree. Before I quite finished it, I was married to Mary Page of Dubuque, and when we took our first real teaching job, we took it at the University of Utah, back where I came from and yearned to return to.

If contentment were the only basis for choice, we might well have chosen to stay there, but I had my father's blood in me, and the habit of moving. Accident was sure to blow me out of any rut I found comfortable. About in October 1936, I started writing a short novel based on a story Mary had told me about her grandfather's Iowa town. By December I had sent it in to a contest that was being sponsored by Little, Brown. In January I got word that I had won the $2,500 prize. That was a lot of money in 1937, to people in our circumstances, and it was shortly doubled by a serial magazine sale. Rich, we took off into the wider world. Why not? I was my father's son.

The summer of 1937 we spent on bicycles in France and England. Coming home broke, we took another teaching job, this time at Wisconsin. Many years later I would write up that experience, fictionalized to taste, in the novel *Crossing to Safety.* But we did not, like the Morgans of that book, end up with dismissal, polio, and a safety-net job in the publishing business. We ended up, after two years, at Harvard, in conformance with our pattern of moving from our center out into wider and wider worlds.

Wider worlds, but with an eye always on the center. At Harvard, lapping up ideas and associations of the kind I had always hungered for, I never forgot who I was or where I came from. In Madison I had written a little jejune novel called *On a Darkling Plain,* trying out fictionally the textures of my Saskatchewan childhood. In Cambridge I wrote, out of sheer nostalgia, the nonfiction

An early placer mine, twenty-five miles west of Bluff, Utah, virtually in the shadow of the balanced rock known locally as Mexican Hat. (Courtesy Special Collections, University of Utah Library)

*Workers cutting and numbering granite blocks for Mormon temples
and homes in Salt Lake City. (Courtesy Utah State Historical Society)*

book *Mormon Country,* and when that was done I sat down seriously to the events that had mattered to me, and wrote *The Big Rock Candy Mountain.* After that, we took the first opportunity to come back West, first living in Santa Barbara while I finished the wartime study of racial and religious minorities called *One Nation,* done in collaboration with *Look* magazine, and then moving to Stanford without ever going back to Cambridge.

By the time we arrived in Palo Alto I was already involved in the biography of John Wesley Powell, the quintessential Westerner, and had committed myself to a lifetime of writing about the West. My childhood was buried in Saskatchewan, my youth and all my dead in Salt Lake City, and I was never going to go back to either of those places to live. Nevertheless I was at home in the region I belonged in, and I thought I had lived outside it long enough to have some perspective on it.

It is a not unusual life curve for Westerners—to live in and be shaped by the bigness, space, clarity, and hopefulness of the West, to go away for study and enlargement and the perspective that distance and dissatisfaction can give, and then to return to where they belong.

Frank Waters. (Photo by Joe Backes)

FRANK WATERS

Frank Waters was born more than eighty-six years ago with a double portion of the drifter already in him. All his life he's been what people in other parts might call a rambling man.

You'd need a large map, moreover, to trace the many places the years of rambling have taken him: New York, Washington, D.C., Mexico City, Los Angeles. Up and down the American West from northern Wyoming to the Arizona border and just about every wide spot on the road in between. Part Indian on his father's side—Cheyenne, he'll tell you—he's spent time in Hopi villages and Ute encampments and Navajo trading posts, crawled around old Mayan ruins in the jungles of Central America and tried to decipher the signs left centuries ago on cliff palaces hidden down the twisting canyons of New Mexico. As an engineer, he's worked in the Imperial Valley and wrestled pipe in the Salt Creek oil fields; a man with a keen and searching mind, he's served his government as its official spokesman in the development and testing of fission atomic bombs in Nevada.

And of course he's been a writer of books. Twice a nominee for the Nobel Prize in literature, awarded six honorary doctoral degrees, and the subject of several seminars devoted to his work, he's considered by some critics, including the respected literary scholar John Milton, to be one of the most distinguished Western writers of the twentieth century.

Yet few among the general public have become familiar enough with his writing to say. His has never been one of the more fashionable literary reputations. Certainly not fashionable on a wide national scale. He's been read, but most often by ethnologists and ecologists, history buffs, appreciators of Western writing—seldom by subway riders or legions of vacationers in their lakeside hammocks. In his almost sixty years of writing, not one of his books has ever come within shouting distance of a best-seller list.

"I had my own good reasons for writing them," Waters says when asked about this, speaking from behind a thin gray garland of pipe smoke. "I suppose I might have liked more people reading my books, but that wouldn't have changed anything. I would have written them all the same way anyway."

You see there is this too about Waters, the thing that makes a day spent with him especially memorable: He doesn't really much care about all that. Not really. Despite the public's long neglect, despite the smallness of the material rewards thrown to him for his considerable creative labors, despite everything that might and probably should have been, he seems a contented man.

Take, for example, an encounter he described having recently with a publisher, a man of some stature in the book community who shall remain, mercifully, nameless.

The fellow came calling on him several years ago with a proposal that sounded very interesting, indeed: He wanted to put out a deluxe, forty-fifth-anniversary edition of Waters's American Indian classic *The Man Who Killed the Deer,* which would be aimed especially at the collector's market, very fancy, with hand-numbered copies and a special cover and illustrations. And Waters told him yes, well, why didn't he put something down on paper and drop it in the mail, so they'd both know exactly what it was they were talking about.

When the contract finally arrived, Waters said, he read it through, casually at first and then more carefully, and could hardly believe what he was seeing.

Frank Waters. (Photo by Joe Backes)

He sent it off to his agent and she couldn't believe it either. It called for almost nothing in the way of author's royalties for him but everything for the publisher, including control of future rights to the book for just about eternity.

It was a sucker deal if you asked him, Waters ventured thoughtfully. The island of Manhattan in exchange for a handshake and a handful of beads all over again.

He smiled, thoroughly enjoying all this. "I put the contract in an envelope and sent it back to the publisher, unsigned," he said. "I don't hold it against him. He's a businessman. I just don't want him doing business on me."

We were sitting in the sunlit living room of his house—not the old, cloud-high one outside Taos with the thirty-inch-thick adobe walls, Waters's primary place-to-come-home-to for the last forty years, but the other one he owns, on the edge of Tucson, where he and his wife Barbara flee for warmth after the first snows of the winter come. It feels, from inside, like an oasis of civilization in a world of Walt Disney cactus and distant mountaintops. There are Navajo patterns on the fabric of the sofa and Hopi kachina dolls (most early and some quite rare) atop the fireplace and a desk backed up to the windows where Waters does his early morning writing. There is a dog asleep on the carpet and fresh coffee in the pot. Above all there are framed works of art—stunning, magnificent art—just about everywhere.

He really understands little about art, Waters says. It was luck and nothing else. Many of the framed pieces turn out to be, on closer inspection, early, unmistakable works by masters of the legendary Taos school: a haunting portrayal of two pueblo women signed by Ernest L. Blumenschein ("Bloomie," Waters calls him; they were good friends), an oil sketch by Leon Gaspard (whose biography Waters wrote a quarter of a century ago), several small studies by Lady Dorothy Brett. The Russian immigrant master Nicolai Fechin did a charcoal portrait of Waters as a young man, and it hangs in an honored place at one end of the room, not far from a relatively recent bronze bust by local artist Mark Rossi. Very, very nice stuff. A museum director's dream.

You and I should only understand art so little.

He has been doing that sort of thing with quiet and unassuming modesty throughout his life: capitalizing on the apparent contradictions in himself. Seeming to go one way, then suddenly achieving something remarkable by turning and going another.

After a commercially unsuccessful novel published when he was twenty-eight titled *Fever Pitch,* a desert adventure filled with the kind of dramatic overkill and panting prose typical of first efforts, Waters looked early to his own experience for subject matter. Over the next ten years he completed three novels—*The Wild Earth's Nobility, Below Grass Roots,* and *Dust Within the Rock*—that tell the continuing, fictionalized story of his maternal grandmother's doomed efforts to find a fabulous "Bowl of Gold" deep in the bowels of Colorado's Pike's Peak. Throughout, the central character's introspective grandson (a thinly disguised portrait of the young Waters himself) broods over this seemingly senseless desecration of a mountain the Indians consider sacred. More than thirty years later Waters was to rewrite all three books and greatly condense them into a single volume published under the title *Pike's Peak: A Colorado Mining Saga,* which some regard as one of the underrated masterworks of Western American literature.

Next he wrote *People of the Valley* and, a year later, *The Man Who Killed the Deer,* considered his two greatest fictional works. Both deal with the struggles of a helpless minority to adopt to the unfeeling forces of progress; in *People of the Valley* the characters are simple Hispanic farmers living in New Mexico's Sangre de Cristo Mountains; in *The Man Who Killed the Deer* they are the Indian residents of an ancient pueblo.

Then followed a virtual grab bag of material: several bulky historical romances, *River Lady* and *Diamond Head* (written quite frankly, he confesses, to lay some nagging bills to rest); a study of the Colorado River for the fine *Rivers of America* series; and biographies of the artist Gaspard and the Earp brothers of Tombstone (actually an as-told-to debunking of the popular Earp myth related by Virgil Earp's widow—Waters's single foray into investigative journalism). He was hired by Hollywood for a lucrative few months to write screenplays for a production company that never quite got off the ground. By 1963 his writing career seemed on the wane.

It was then, after four years of intensive labor, that his nonfiction *Book of the Hopi* was published, today arguably his best-known work. In it Waters the man of science turned to a subject that could be called science's opposite—the "right-brain" or nonlogical approach to everyday life practiced by the reclusive Hopi Indians—to reveal as no one had before the heart and soul of pre-Columbian American civilization. It was a landmark work, and is still required reading in many university anthropology courses. Twelve years later he extended his study in another book, which he called *Mexico Mystique,* a look at the mystical and religious beliefs of the Toltec, Aztec, and Mayan Indians.

The really amazing thing is that all these books are still in print, Waters points out proudly. If you care enough to put a little effort into it, you can still find and buy a brand-new copy of every book he has ever written—twenty-two of them, stretching back over more than half a century. How many other writers today—or ever—can match that? Barbara, an attractive, outgoing blond woman much younger than her husband, nods idly in agreement from the sofa where she is sitting, having apparently heard this several times before. Their relationship is a close one; she is openly devoted to him.

But it was after four o'clock. My gosh, Waters said, he hadn't noticed; the birds would be getting impatient for their daily handout. With surprising agility he propelled his lanky, six-foot-one-inch frame from his chair and headed out back.

The birds were indeed there, dozens and dozens of them, wild and quite vocally free: cardinals, woodpeckers, Gambel's quails, red-tailed hawks, Inca doves, thrashers, hummingbirds, and God only knows what else. Waiting in unaccustomed fraternity in and around a small garden just beyond Waters's back door. He filled both hands and began spreading the treats around.

He was smiling as he worked. Not broadly, but perceptibly. A reflection of some inner sense of calm, undoubtedly. And his total absorption in what he was doing.

You can mark that down as something any Westerner would understand: how to be all alone in the whole wide world, and still be a happy man.

C.B., 1987

The Changing and Unchangeable West

Mountain-bred, I was born at the foot of Pike's Peak in Colorado Springs, Colorado, in 1902. The small, sedate town of thirty thousand residents, popularly called Little London, was a noted scenic resort and health spa that drew visitors from all over the country. No liquor was sold within the city limits, and the Sunday newspaper refrained from including a comic section because it might keep children from attending Sunday school.

Our neighborhood didn't lie in the rich and fashionable North End but along Bijou Street and Shook's Run, where we gathered watercress. Life was never dull. The Pan Dandy bread wagon stopped at our house early every morning. It was drawn by a fast pair of sorrel mares, and in the winter my younger sister and I hitched our sled behind it for an exciting ride to Columbia School. In the summer we waited for the arrival of the ice wagon—its driver would chip off pieces of ice for us to suck through our handkerchiefs—and the knife-and-scissors sharpener, who set up his portable grinding stone on the curb.

These visitors didn't deter us from shopping at the corner grocery store, where we always were given a dill pickle from the barrel and often sent home with a free slab of "easy meat," or liver. An ice-cream cone cost a buffalo nickel, a licorice stick an Indian penny. The standard coin of the realm was a silver

*A peaceful summer afternoon in Colorado Springs shortly after the turn of the
century. (Margaretta Boas photo, courtesy Pike's Peak Library District)*

dollar minted in Denver from Colorado-mined silver. No greenbacks, please.

High, snowy Pike's Peak dominated our earliest years. We learned early to foretell the weather from it. The usual Sunday outing for my sister and me was a streetcar ride with Father and Mother to Manitou Springs, six miles west. Here, at the base of the peak, we filled our bottles with iron-and-soda water gushing from the many springs. Often we rented a burro, or "Pike's Peak canary," from one of the crowded corrals to carry us children and our picnic basket up a mountain canyon threaded by a turbulent white-water stream.

My first ride on a train ended in a disaster. My father was taking us to Denver on the Denver & Rio Grande line. I was sitting in the coach, nose flattened against the window. Near Husted, a few miles north of our boarding point, I watched another train coming toward us around a curve. Then suddenly I was on the floor amid a jumble of baggage and overturned seats and a bedlam of shrieks and groans. The two trains had collided headlong.

Father got us out of the wreck to sit on the prairie under mother's umbrella. Around us all afternoon lay other passengers, injured and dying. Doctors and nurses came driving out from Colorado Springs. Their help was generally refused upon the advice of railroad officials, because no medical fees or insurance would be paid to those who didn't wait for the railroad's own doctors. They finally came.

My left arm evidently had been injured. Throughout the winter mother dutifully took me to the railroad doctor, who was unable to help me. To ease the constant pain I kept rubbing my forearm until it developed a growth. That spring, when I was in seventh grade, I broke the arm while playing baseball. That healed it as medical treatment couldn't.

An exciting event during those years was the lightweight championship fight between Freddie Welsh and Charlie White held in Colorado Springs one afternoon in 1914. I didn't watch it. I was the Fred Harvey newsboy at the new Santa Fe railroad station. But late that afternoon, while special trains were

A group of Colorado Springs ladies on a day's outing gather at Halfway House on Barr Trail high above Manitou Springs in 1915. (Courtesy local history collection, Pike's Peak Library District)

filling with the returning crowd of fight spectators, a truckload of newspaper extras arrived headlining double news. Freddie Welsh had won the championship, and during the bout the flimsy wooden stands had collapsed, injuring dozens of fans. Everybody screamed for a paper, thrusting quarters and dollars into my hand until my pockets bulged. It was my most profitable day.

Jack Dempsey, born in Colorado, was of course our boyhood idol. On the memorable Fourth of July, 1919, when he KO'd Jess Willard to gain the world's heavyweight championship, I stood in the immense crowd on Pike's Peak Avenue in front of the *Gazette* building. From a second-story window an announcer with a megaphone, reading the telegraphic dispatches handed him, called out every blow.

Beautiful and sedate as it usually was, Little London owed its imposing mansions in the North End not to the English money and taste that had laid out the town but to Cripple Creek, on the eleven-thousand-foot-high south slope of Pike's Peak. Gold had been discovered there as late as 1891; the "Cripple Creek Cow Pasture" quickly became the world's greatest gold camp, eventually producing some $450 million in gold at the then current rate of twenty-one dollars an ounce.

The pharmacist at our corner drugstore rushed up there on a Sunday morning, threw his hat in a gulch and dug where it fell. Thus was discovered the rich Pharmacist Mine. Jimmie Burns, a plumber, found an even richer vein, from which he extracted enough gold to build the new Burns Theater. Everybody was getting rich.

My grandfather Joseph Dozier, a prosperous pioneer building contractor, also succumbed to gold fever. He persuaded my father to help him open a series of exploratory tunnels. I often rode up there with them—a mile straight up and eighteen miles west—on the spectacular Cripple Creek Short Line Railroad.

Cripple Creek was everything conservative Little London wasn't. It was a madhouse of activity and extravagant hopes. The muddy roads between its major towns, Cripple Creek and Victor, were crowded with mule-drawn freight and ore wagons; muckers and drillers elbowed promoters and stockbrokers on every corner; ladies in long skirts and high-button shoes were jostled off board sidewalks by the prostitutes from Myer's Avenue. How exciting it was!

Grandfather and Grandmother often talked about Winfield Scott Stratton, whose discovery of the famous Independence Mine had opened the district. For seventeen winters he had worked for Grandfather as a journeyman carpenter, saving his wages to grubstake his prospecting through the summers. Destiny finally rewarded his persistence with the Independence, which he sold for ten million dollars before he died.

The "Midas of the Rockies" didn't forget his lean years. He devoted his great wealth to town improvements and to establish the Myron Stratton Home for old, impoverished prospectors who had never struck it rich.

That Stratton had become a hopeless alcoholic and recluse didn't diminish Grandfather's hopes. None of his own workings ever struck pay dirt. He eventually lost all he owned except his house, whose title was in Grandmother's name. But still he borrowed money to open another unproductive mine, our Family Folly, the Sylvanite.

My father, Jonathan, was a man of space, not height, of open plains, not mountains. He was part Indian, Cheyenne. One of his best friends was an Indian vegetable huckster named Joe. Father often rode around with him on his rounds. The sight of Father, neatly dressed in a suit and polished boots, sitting on the plank seat of a rickety wagon beside an Indian huddled in a tattered blanket always infuriated Mother. She was even more disconcerted by father's visits to the Ute encampment.

The Utes had been moved to a reservation farther west, but a band of them was permitted to return every summer to their former homeland nearby. Their encampment of smoke-gray lodges lay on a mesa just west of town.

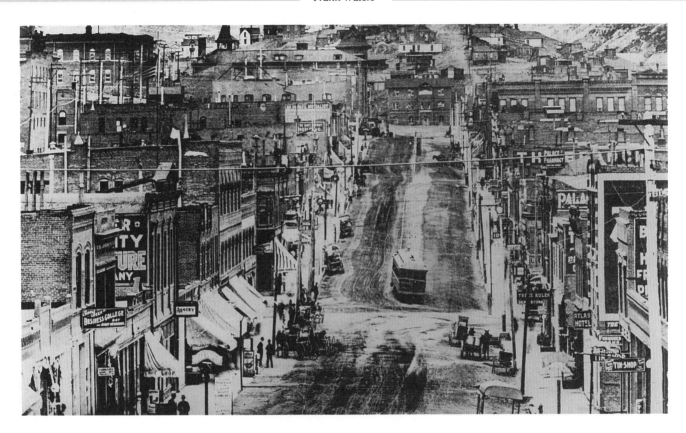

*Cripple Creek's Bennett Avenue at the height of the gold boom
in 1903, when the town's population reached thirty thousand.
(Courtesy Western History Department, Denver Public Library)*

*A makeshift diner advertises its prices in the early days
of the Cripple Creek gold rush. (Photo by W. E. Hook,
courtesy of the Colorado Historical Society)*

Respectable Little London avoided it, but Father frequently took me there of an evening. He would squat down cross-legged in the circle of men around the cooking fire. With the long-bladed knife he always carried, even to church, he would cut off a pink slice of steaming meat from the fire and eat it, as did they, in his fingers. I waited patiently with the women and children outside the circle for my turn at table.

The high peak rising above us was the Utes' sacred mountain, looming prominently in their creation myth. It had power. As they talked about it their dark, wrinkled faces in the flame light seemed to possess an inner glow. It darkened as they haltingly voiced their fears of how the mountain was being violated by the open trenches, glory holes, and abandoned tunnels and shafts. "This mountain sick," one of the elders ventured. "Pretty soon it lose all its power."

One summer Father took me with him to New Mexico to live for a time in the remote trading post of Hon-Not-Klee, "Shallow Water," in the immense Navajo reservation. My first impression of the trading post was of an island in a vast pelagic plain, a fortress in an empty wilderness.

The building was a thick-walled adobe with iron-barred windows. Its huge trading room was full of goods: salt and sugar and coffee, canned goods, bridles and ropes, bolts of flowered gingham and brilliant velveteen. In back were our living quarters, a storeroom for sheep pelts and huge sacks of Navajo wool, and a double-locked rug room piled with gorgeous Navajo blankets and exquisite Navajo silver-and-turquoise jewelry, which had been brought in for pawn or trade.

The master of this outpost, supplying the needs of perhaps a thousand square miles, was a man named Bruce. He was ill, and Father had come to help him manage the post, the Navajos' only contact with an alien, encroaching people.

All day they rode in—slim, arrogant men on horseback, women and children huddled in springless wagons. They impressed me with their independence, their air of barbarity, their love of color, and their reverence for the earth, their mother.

This was a natural life for my father. Bruce wanted him to stay, but he was recalled home to work with Grandfather in Cripple Creek and died shortly thereafter.

Times and customs by then were changing. Men's high stiff collars went out of fashion, and their Paris garters gave way to stretch socks. Uniformity decreed that I part my hair in the middle and plaster it down with Vaseline. I bought my first safety razor and waited impatiently for the time to use it.

My first fledgling flight from home carried me to Wyoming. I had worked my way through high school and three years in Colorado College as an engineering major before I realized I wasn't cut out to be an engineer. Leaving school, I rode the train to Casper, then hitchhiked a ride with a truck driver to the booming Salt Creek oil fields. There I got a job as a roustabout with a gang laying ten-inch iron pipe. For hitting the hooks all day we were paid fifty cents an hour. In turn we paid fifty cents each for breakfast and supper, and another fifty cents for the use of a cot in the bunkhouse. Lunch out on the prairie was simple and free, sandwiches and apples.

On Saturday nights we trudged five miles into the squatter town of Lavoye to spend our remaining wages for bootleg beer. With their two-story fronts of unpainted wood, Lavoye's ramshackle buildings looked like a movie set. Swarming with men, trucks, and machinery, all Salt Creek reminded me of Cripple Creek. The jackpot of one was gold, the other oil.

That fall of 1924 I met an old-time Westerner who had been a trapper, horse wrangler, and cowpuncher, and had worked as a guide for one of Theodore Roosevelt's Western jaunts. He had been offered a home with his

A view of the Salt Creek oil fields near Casper, Wyoming, about 1922.
(Courtesy Western Historical Collection, University of Colorado)

daughter in California. With his savings he had bought a little Star roadster to drive there but had difficulty driving it. He persuaded me to drive him. "You won't have to buy an overcoat to wear in sunny California," he assured me. "And whenever you get hungry, all you'll have to do is pick oranges off the trees along every street."

We drove south through Wyoming and Colorado, then west through New Mexico and Arizona on U.S. Route 66, with frequent stops to change tires and cool the radiator. Many stretches of dirt road were unmarked and unfenced. Every evening we turned off to camp in the sage. What a wide, empty land! There were no large cities. Santa Fe was a little town of eleven thousand people and narrow cobblestone streets. Albuquerque's population was thirty-five thousand. The largest city in the Southwest was Phoenix, housing barely fifty thousand residents.

Along the way we passed through many Indian pueblos. The people in each were differently dressed, spoke their own tongue, and observed their own customs. Far to the north stretched the vast Navajo country I'd seen with my father. All this heartland of America's Indian country would become intimately familiar to me later.

Puttering along at thirty miles an hour, we finally topped the desert mountains above the old Arizona mining town of Oatman. Below us lay the muddy Colorado River. Beyond it and the Mojave Desert was the Promised Land.

The City of the Angels was a shocking disappointment. We drove into what the old cowboy remembered as the center of the city—the historic Mexican plaza at the north end of Main Street. In this shabby neighborhood of adobe buildings there were no orange trees. We divided our last few dollars, and he drove on to his daughter's house near San Diego, while I rented for four dollars a week a room in a squalid hotel on the plaza.

From its grimy window there was no sign of the blue Pacific. I had yet to discover uptown a newer, more modern Los Angeles, or to find a job. But none of this belittled my great accomplishment. I had crossed the entire breadth of the American West and reached the last frontier city on the ocean's shore, the ultimate goal of that Manifest Destiny that had impelled America's westward expansion.

Imperial Valley, on the California–Baja California border, where I was sent some time later to work as a junior engineer by the telephone company, lay 235 feet below sea level in the heart of the Colorado Desert. Mountain-bred, I was fascinated by the desert's tawny, treeless expanse under the pitiless sun. Yuma, Arizona, lay on the bank of the Colorado River to the east; water from there was channeled to the sea-level fields on the boundary of Mexico, whence it drained down into Imperial Valley.

Under irrigation, the valley's desert floor had become "America's Winter Garden," producing that year fourteen thousand train carloads of cantaloupes. Already by May 1 the first melons to reach the East's breakfast tables had been shipped. The little towns with their large packing sheds bustled with activity in desert heat of 106 degrees. All the valley seemed to be a boom camp resembling Cripple Creek and Salt Creek, its own symbol a round, ripe cantaloupe.

In El Centro, the largest town, the lobby of the Barbara Worth Hotel—named for Harold Bell Wright's popular, sentimental novel *The Winning of Barbara Worth*—was the focus of activity. Murals on the walls pictured scenes from the novel, and the hotel stationery and dining room silver carried portraits of the young lady herself under a fetching sombrero. Here thronged fruit brokers telephoning Kansas City, Chicago, and New York to order diversions of refrigerator boxcars as the market rose and fell with the thermometer. Ranchers in heavy boots stomped in, demanding trucks, railroad cars, more

Packing along the Sturdevant Trail in Angeles National Forest,
California. (Courtesy California State Library, Sacramento)

workmen. As a young engineer I was kept busy following all this activity, meeting the demand for efficient telephone service from overworked switchboards.

Yet in all the valley the place that intrigued me most was Mexicali, the Mexican border town adjoining the American town of Calexico—perhaps because it seemed so blatantly to manifest the dark, repressed domain in our Puritan-Anglo soul.

Mexicali was the bottom of the human barrel. Its portals were the Owl and the Southern Club, two great casinos offering bars, dining and gaming rooms, music and entertainment. To them every evening came the melon growers, brokers, well-heeled ranchers, and businessmen looking for a bit of fun. At nine o'clock the whistle blew for their exodus back across the international line. The gates clanged shut then. The lights went out.

Down the back streets beyond the two casinos lay ill-lit cantinas with names such as El Gato Negro, Tivoli, and Casa Blanca, and nameless dirt-floor drinking dens selling mescal and green tequila. And behind them were their cribs—open courtyards holding twenty or more shapeless women apiece in sweaty shifts. The alcoholic stench and acrid odor of urine filled the desert night.

Now was their hour. As if from deep underground emerged the petty criminals and refugees of both countries: pimps and prostitutes; all the mixtures of Indian, Mexican, and Anglo breeds—mestizos, coyotes, criollos, *cholos;* crawling beggars; Negro cotton pickers; giant Hindus with heads swathed in black turbans; Chinese hopheads. The barrio wasn't a safe place for the unwary. The women in any crib could strip you of your clothes in an instant, and a knife might be stuck in your back when you turned a dark corner.

Despite the savage brutality and perversions, I began to feel that all this teeming life, not yet informed with the qualities that mark more evolved human forms, does indeed gush up from a mysterious wellspring of all life, ever replenishing humankind with its brute strength and fresh vitality. This feeling, I must admit, may have been nourished by Tai Ling, the yogi of Cockroach Court.

He had been among the first of the Chinese who had been imported by shiploads to work in the great cotton fields south of the border, congregating here in a Chinese quarter that equaled in fact the storied Barbary Coast. It was known as La Plaza de las Cucarachas, "Cockroach Court," named for its swarming prostitutes called cucarachas.

Here stood Tai Ling's shop. He sat behind his abacus at the front window, a small man wearing a black sateen jacket and ragged trousers. I struck up a friendship with him and visited him often.

His shop was cluttered with barrels of rice, pinto beans and garbanzos, strips of dried meat, rolls of matting, packets and jars of lily roots, lichee nuts, herbs, silk panties, and American blue-denim trousers. Twice a week he distributed fresh fish brought up from the gulf. He marked and sold Chinese lottery tickets, and peddled cans of Rooster and Elephant–brand opium. His dark cellar, I found out, served as a station on the underground line that smuggled Chinese workers across the international border to Los Angeles's Chinatown and thence to San Francisco.

Tai Ling also traveled another, more difficult road. As a struggling yogi, he followed the path to spiritual illumination by meditating on the divine and undefinable, unbounded and indivisible Ultimate Reality, the Tao. He saw no conflict between his two paths, for as a yogi he accepted good and evil as equal parts of the universal whole and was partial to neither. He was an incomprehensible character whose magnetism kept drawing me back to him, but I could never quite make him out. Perhaps this is why, of all the important people I met in the Imperial Valley, to this day it is he I remember most vividly.

QUONG HOP SING
& CO.
735

廣合成

A Chinese businessman waits on a customer outside his shop in California shortly after the turn of the century. (Courtesy California State Library, Sacramento)

How different was the beautiful blue valley of Mora as I knew it several years later. I was no longer working at a salaried job and had come to write my first long novel in the valley's peace and seclusion. It was a world apart, tucked in the high Sangre de Cristo mountains of northern New Mexico. To drive to the nearest large town—Las Vegas, New Mexico, scarcely thirty miles south—took two hours, and the road over the pass to Taos was impassable a good part of the year.

The valley had first been occupied in 1835 by seventy-six Spanish colonial settlers from Mexico. Their descendants still spoke their mother tongue, adhered to their Spanish traditions, and worked their small family fields for a meager living.

Mora was the central village, surrounded by tiny settlements of a dozen or so houses in the enclosing mountains. During my two years there I lived in a rambling, eighteen-room adobe hacienda known as the Butler Hotel. It was without plumbing, furnished with walnut-spool feather beds and wardrobes brought from the officers' quarters of abandoned Fort Union.

The hotel was owned by a middle-aged woman, Sybil Butler. Her husband, Monte, had been a professional gambler who had fled there from Indian territory with a price on his head. Going blind, he had taken in a half-Cherokee named Ralph, also a refugee from the law. Monte patiently taught Ralph how to deal cards and all the other tricks of the gambler's trade. Now, after old blind Monte had died, Ralph stayed on, running the hotel for Mrs. Butler. His only earnings were his winnings from the poker games he conducted every night for passing cattle buyers, surveyors, and occasional state officials.

The only other permanent guests beside myself were a couple, Fran and Ed Tinker. One of their two rooms was a kitchen. I took supper with them there, because Mrs. Butler only cooked breakfast before retiring to her own room for the rest of the day.

Ed was a black sheep, part Osage Indian, whose brother was the famous major general shot down at Midway (Tinker Airfield in Oklahoma City is named after him). A handsome six-footer, Ed dabbled in local politics, occasionally rebuilt a washed-out bridge, and generally relied on his wife's wages.

Fran, a woman whose small stature and unassuming manner gave no evidence of her resoluteness and capability, was one of the most remarkable people I've ever known. Her father had been a judge in Santa Fe, and she spoke colloquial Spanish as fluently as English. Her job—part of the federal Work Projects Administration program—was to teach families in these remote canyons to use pressure cookers to preserve meat, vegetables, and fruit for winter instead of drying them in the sun, but other problems always confronted her. I often accompanied her on her rounds, impressed by her abilities and her compassion as she delivered babies, broke fevers, and taught the medicinal uses of native herbs and plants.

I loved them both.

My only other friend of non-Hispanic stock, who readily joked with me in English, was Peter Balland. A one-legged Frenchman, he and his family ran the general-merchandise store opposite the hotel. He was a shrewd trader. When an impoverished family had run up a bill it couldn't pay, he would stomp on his wooden leg to their dirt-floored adobe and take down from their wall the painted image *(santo)* or carved wooden figure *(bulto)* of a Christian saint. "I will just take this in payment for your debt," he would say. "Now you will have no more worry about it, no?"

These old, primitive, and rare santos and bultos covered the walls of his rear butcher shop. He kept offering them for sale to the museum and university in Santa Fe, with no success. Eventually his collection was taken to the Fine

Arts Center in Colorado Springs, which showed it in traveling exhibitions throughout the country.

These were my fellow passengers on what, during winter especially, seemed like a ship becalmed in a protected harbor, undisturbed by the waves of outer change. Past my window ebbed the earthy people of the valley, going to mass or market. Theirs was still the life that had given the Southwest its distinctive Spanish culture, projected from the past into the present.

But already a storm was gathering outside.

The development of the first atom bomb on Los Alamos mesa northwest of Santa Fe, and its detonation in the desert of southern New Mexico, changed all our lives, the entire world. It ushered in the Atomic Age.

I had served a short stint in the army at the beginning of World War II before being released to write analyses of events in Latin America for the Office of Inter-American Affairs. Soon after the war ended, Russia unexpectedly exploded its own first atom bomb, then another war began in Korea. Under the threat of these events the Los Alamos Scientific Laboratory began developing a series of new fission bombs, which increased the explosive power of its first A-bomb tenfold. These new nuclear weapons were tested in the desert sixty miles north of Las Vegas, Nevada.

I accepted the offer of a job as information consultant at the laboratory. I worked at Los Alamos during the winter, and each spring accompanied the scientists to Nevada for the test series. From their control point, a huge block-house, I witnessed the awesome detonation of almost a hundred bombs in the "Valley Where the Giant Mushrooms Grow"—a searing experience I can neither forget nor describe.

When I finally resigned to return home and resume my life at the typewriter, I became aware of what had been happening elsewhere. The entire

West was undergoing developments that would change its face forever.

Precious uranium, the life force of the Atomic Age, had been discovered in New Mexico. It opened the entire West to the greatest prospecting rush since the scramble for gold of the century before. Men carrying Geiger counters were penetrating deep mountain canyons, plodding through empty deserts, and across the immense Colorado Plateau. The last undeveloped area in the nation held the greatest uranium deposits in the world. Six hundred mines were producing ore; mills were going up. Little villages I had once known were suddenly thriving towns; cities were expanding miles outward and bursting with prosperity.

In my own middle life I went to the dead center of this maelstrom of activity, to live for almost three years among the Hopi Indians in northern Arizona. It was the perfect counterpoint to the events swirling about me, a period of personal introspection as rewarding as the perspective on the outer world I had gained.

I had written in 1942 a novel of pueblo life, *The Man Who Killed the Deer,* and in 1951 a nonfiction study of Navajo and Pueblo Indian ceremonialism, *Masked Gods.* Both had reflected my empathy with Indians and my study of their lives, but neither had broken through the traditional secrecy that veiled the Indians' innermost religious beliefs from outside observers. Now, another decade later, I began writing a third book, *Book of the Hopi,* which would give the Hopis' own account of their creation myth and continental migrations and explain the esoteric meanings of their annual nine great ceremonies—the only true indigenous mystery plays in America.

Such a book would break new ground. The Hopis always had been considered the most secretive of all tribes and a puzzle to a generation of rational white anthropologists and ethnologists, who couldn't fathom the aura of myth and mysticism enshrouding them.

While gathering information for the book I lived at Pumpkin Seed Point,

The village of Shongopovi. Glass-plate photos such as this one are rare
for a time when Hopis regarded both cameras and visitors with suspicion.
(Courtesy Western Historical Collection, University of Colorado)

overlooking New Oraibi on Third Mesa, in a little house without plumbing, heated by a butane gas stove and lit by a kerosene lamp. I took my meals at the nearby house of my Hopi research assistant and interpreter, Oswald White Bear Fredericks, and his white wife.

The Hopis claimed to be the first inhabitants of this New World, the fourth successive world they had occupied. Disputed as this claim was by anthropologists, their pueblo of Oraibi, dating from A.D. 1100 or earlier, was admittedly the oldest continuously occupied settlement in the United States. Unlike the nomadic Navajos, they were a sedentary people who occupied, in all, just nine villages or pueblos on top of three rocky mesas a hundred miles north of the small white towns along U.S. Route 66. Their patches of corn, beans, and squash lay in the sandy desert below. Without irrigation, they depended upon their prayerful ceremonials to bring infrequent rain.

I was fortunate in gaining the confidence of thirty of them, who related to me their world view and the esoteric meanings of their rituals. They spoke willingly, wanting to leave for their children and grandchildren a record of their people's beliefs. Most of them were older men and women. I still in sleepless hours of the night see their dark, wrinkled faces and gnarled hands, hear their low measured voices that seemed to rise out of the depths of an archaic America we have never known, out of a fathomless racial unconscious.

One of the first I met was an aging man in a ragged red sweater and baggy pants, whose straggly gray hair fell to his shoulders. He was Dan Qochhongva, religious leader of Hotevilla Pueblo. His father, Chief Yukioma, had once been dubbed the American Dalai Lama and jailed for seventeen years by the government Indian agent for inciting the Hopi Traditionalists, or "Hostiles," against the Progressives, or "Friendlies," who had welcomed the incoming white people.

Old Dan first viewed me with suspicion. "If your heart is right and you are sincere, you will have four dreams," he concluded. One by one they came to me, as I have related elsewhere, resulting in his sponsoring my research. I hadn't yet witnessed the Hopi ceremonials, nor did I know their meanings. But each successive dream symbolically, as it were, initiated me into them before they took place.

Old Dan I saw frequently. Although I couldn't understand Hopi any better than he could understand English, our curious relationship continued until I left.

My closest Hopi companion was John Lansa of Oraibi. Seventy years old, alert and tireless, he tended a flock of sheep that provided his livelihood. He was head of the Badger clan, which controlled the important Niman kachina ceremony. He took me with him on one of his arduous pilgrimages to gather spruce for the rituals, and accompanied White Bear and me to Mesa Verde and Chaco Canyon, homes of the long-ago Indian cliff dwellers. Not only could he speak good English, he was also able to read the ancient petroglyphs on the cliff walls.

Mina Lansa, his small, frail wife, was the adopted daughter of Chief Tewaquaptewa of Oraibi and custodian of the Bear clan sacred tablets, the ancient Hopi titles to their land. The old chief died while I was there, leaving no Bear-clan successor. His position of *kikmongwi* reverted by right of clan succession to Mina's Parrot clan. She thus became the symbolic mother of the Hopis, as Tewaquaptewa had been their father.

She also became the leader of the Traditionalists, the former "Hostiles," who were opposed to the modern "Friendlies," now dominated by the federal government's Bureau of Indian Affairs. With failing strength she fought the bureau's ever-growing control of tribal matters until she died. John remained my close friend, visiting me in Taos and Tucson until he, too, died years later.

The intimacy I shared with White Bear and his wife helped to carry our project to a successful end. But it was the thirty elderly Hopis who finally

*Hopi Indians eat from the communal bowl, in their
ancient tribal village of Shongopovi. (Courtesy Western
Historical Collection, University of Colorado)*

opened to me the door to all Indian America, a world that once extended unbroken from Central America up through Mexico and the American Southwest, and which still endured here on the Hopi mesas.

What separated Hopi life from our own Anglo culture wasn't ethnic differences, but modes of thinking. Accepting Robert Ornstein's current explanation, we Anglos, being predominantly concerned with the material aspects of the world, rely almost wholly upon the rational, intellectual function of the human brain's left cerebral hemisphere. From our first arrival on this continent we have viewed the land as a vast treasure house of inanimate nature to be plundered at will. The Indians, on the other hand, from pre-Columbian times, were geared to the brain's right hemisphere, which controls intuitional and spiritual perceptions, reflecting their holistic orientation in space and time.

Whatever the reason, the Hopis were the last island of Indian America not yet submerged in the ocean of Anglo materialism. They still existed in a realm whose elements were dream, myth, and mysticism. To them the earth was their living mother. Stones, stars, the corn plant and the spruce, all birds and animals, the locust and the ant, were likewise imbued with a universal inner spirit as well as a physical form. One did not kill a deer or fell a lofty pine without first ritually asking its consent to its sacrifice for the good of all. The spiritual components of these things remained alive as sources of psychical energy, manifesting themselves during ceremonials as masked kachinas.

The nine great annual ceremonials with their symbolism, rituals, dances, songs, and prayers unfolded like stages of consciousness expanding to a vision of universal unity. They seemed to me to be as soundly conceived and executed as the scientific processes developed at Los Alamos, meant not to test a hypothesis of releasable physical energy from divisible matter but to assert a thousand-year-old belief in the indestructibility of the spiritual energy that informs all inert matter and breathing forms. Here on the Hopi mesas I found the indigenous culture of America, still preserving those transcendent values of universal wholeness and unity so desperately needed by our fragmented world today.

Now my heart's home base, as it has been for almost forty years, is my adobe house and back pastures in the Sangre de Cristo mountains of northern New Mexico. It repeats features important to me in my past: Pike's Peak has been replaced by the Sacred Mountain of Taos Pueblo, a horseback ride through the pueblo reservation. The ceremonial dances here are among the best in the Rio Grande pueblos, and the religious leaders have been my close friends for many years.

The little village of Arroyo Seco, a mile down the dirt road, is as wholly Spanish as is Mora, and a century older. It once had the reputation of harboring *brujas,* or witches, as well as horse thieves and other offenders escaping the clutches of the sheriff. When I first settled here, despite the extravagant tales of witchcraft and wickedness matching the actual evils once found in Mexicali, I was the only Anglo in the vicinity. I found it conservatively peaceful, and my neighbors have always looked after me.

My wife Barbara and I, taking our evening walk up the mountain slope, can see the twinkling lights of Los Alamos. I think of the friendly, peace-loving scientists I worked with there and in Nevada, the men who achieved the release of atomic energy, only to have it used today as an agent that threatens the obliteration of all mankind. The sky is darkening with pollutants and particulates drifting here from the Four Corners area to the west. There huge power plants and the strip-mining monsters of powerful energy corporations are exploiting the land as ruthlessly as did the men at Cripple Creek, Salt Creek, and the Imperial Valley.

Change. Constant change is the law of life. Everything is different, yet everything is the same. The American West reflects this paradox. It shows the ever-changing present, and somehow embodies an eternal existence at the same time. We can hope that, as the Hopis say, the spirit that imbues the land will outlast the change.

A driver takes a rest break on the plank road that stretches across the sun-scorched Southwestern desert. (Courtesy Western Historical Collection, University of Colorado)

A Note on the Type

The text of this book was set in a face called Cheltenham, designed by the architect Bertram Grosvenor Goodhue in collaboration with Ingalls Kimball of The Cheltenham Press of New York. Cheltenham was introduced in the early twentieth century, a period of remarkable achievement in type design. The idea of creating a "family" of types by making variations on the basic type design was originated by Goodhue and Kimball in the design of the Cheltenham series.

Composed by ComCom,
Division of Haddon Craftsmen, Inc.,
Allentown, Pennsylvania

Printed and bound by The Murray Printing Company,
Westford, Massachusetts

Designed by Anthea Lingeman